Poet
Motion

Touring The UK Vol II

Edited by Claire Tupholme

YoungWriters
First published in Great Britain in 2004 by:
Young Writers
Remus House
Coltsfoot Drive
Peterborough
PE2 9JX
Telephone: 01733 890066
Website: www.youngwriters.co.uk

SB ISBN 1 84460 417 9

Foreword

This year, the Young Writers' 'Poetry In Motion' competition proudly presents a showcase of the best poetic talent selected from over 40,000 up-and-coming writers nationwide.

Young Writers was established in 1991 to promote the reading and writing of poetry within schools and to the youth of today. Our books nurture and inspire confidence in the ability of young writers and provide a snapshot of poems written in schools and at home by budding poets of the future.

The thought effort, imagination and hard work put into each poem impressed us all and the task of selecting poems was a difficult but nevertheless enjoyable experience.

We hope you are as pleased as we are with the final selection and that you and your family continue to be entertained with *Poetry In Motion Touring The UK Vol II* for many years to come.

Contents

The Poems

The Knife

A dark winter's night, with a clear full moon,
They are coming, they will arrive soon.
The church was dark, empty and haunted,
Like an old ghost house, that people had taunted.

Surrounding the building, were those which were dead,
Put under the soil, by the shovels in the shed.
There were no gravestones but plenty of loose earth,
The bodies had been put there, by those who were cursed.

Time is running out, their next kill is due soon,
The only witness, is the silence of the moon,
The trees saw it happen, the knife pierce the skin,
But now the same torture is about to begin.

Their shoes are silent, on the grass of the graveyard,
Their whole appearance, is a shivering sort of hard.
They have guns with no conscience and more than a six shot,
They commit many murders, care? They do not.

They near the victim, with one missing thumb,
One pulled out a knife, his hand was numb,
The weapon was sharp, a nine inch blade,
Then suddenly the knife, came out of the shade.

An unbearable agony, blood starting to ooze,
Down, down, onto those cold, black shoes,
Red was blood, that came from your back,
Then your vision turns to black.

They bury your body, with the spades from the shed,
The clothes on your corpse, are stained from the blood shed,
They dump you in a hole with all the worms and creatures,
With slimy, disgusting, sickly features.

You had not paid them back, you hadn't a job
Like all the other corpses, he had messed with the mob.

Emmiline Cambridge (12)

I Am

I am a famous basketball player,
slam-dunking the hoop I am
running up the court with the
fans screaming my name.

I am a pro BMXer going up
the ramp and I pull off the
best trick - a tailwhip, the
crowd love it, they're screaming
for my autograph.

I am a formula 1 racer,
I am in the lead, zooming round
corners, yes my fastest lap.

I am a boxer, punching my
opponent, ouch! that hurt me,
uppercut, yes. I win by a
KO.

I am Ben Doherty, class 8B2
in English. God, when will this bell ring?

Ben Doherty (11)

Hidden Treasure

Down below, my hidden treasure
Goes as far as the eye can see
Where the ocean breeze is calm and cool
It's a big giant fishing pool
The question goes, what on earth is in it?
What it beholds or what it is
Should I touch it or leave it alone?
Is it kind and nice or gives you a groan?
No matter whatever, no matter anyhow
It lives with me forever, for now.

Sheun Oshinbolu (11)

Missundaztood

Full of hate
And full of greed
Among the flowers
Is an ugly weed

Different to them
Can't you see?
Different to you
This is me

Feeling missundaztood
Looking lost and confused
Brain turning off
Mind is abused

Looking at me
Looking back at you
You can't see inside
You don't have a clue.

Tara Stockdale (15)

Trapped

A person staring,
A wolf howling,
Trees rustling,
A baby mouthing.

A lion's roar,
A fish's escape,
Giant jaws widen,
Monkeys and apes.

Rock in the mountains,
Coal in the fire,
My sister screaming,
Birds flying higher.

Kate Whiting (13)

Injustice

We are all the same
We are all as one
All the world
Bad thoughts be gone
But it's not like that
Not for real
White or black, big or small
There's something they don't feel
They say I'm different
I don't fit in
They say he's different
Cos of the colour of his skin
But when you insult
And show no respect
For the whole world
Your actions reflect
Just because you're different
No need to feel shame
Just be your own person
You'll never be the same
Not until they listen
And bad feelings have gone
Let's stand together
The world be one.

Kimberley Abbotts (14)

Untitled

When we wake on Christmas morning
What a lovely sight we see
So many lovely presents beneath the Christmas tree
Then we look out the window
And see the white soft snow
We think of the very first Christmas, a long, long time ago.

Charlie Louise Everett (15)

Wonderchild

Fever burning
Whispered face
Time on time's mist; I wonder you.

Who you? Where you? Why you?
My flesh's fruit
Flickered light that weaves and dances
Half-told secrets
Wonderchild

Like the morning's summer light
And grass and wind and memory till
Memory forgets
That blood and bones and sweat and tears did mingle with the earth
Some ancient battlefield is born again in light and daisy
And twilight mellowness

Fireflies and buttercups and water's path
Do these compare with you – the babe who cries and wails and grows
and dies?
Live again in children and children's children
In time on time's mist
In suffering and pain and beauty

In time on time be reborn
Be life.

Laura Rigby (15)

The School Bully

I saw her the other day staring me in the eye,
She has always been bullying me, I just can't make out why!
I'm too scared to tell a soul even though I should,
She makes me too scared to stand up to her, I wish o wish I would!
Pushing me, pulling my hair,
She acts like a vicious bear,
Growling and snarling she lifts her fist,
I have thoughts about acting back, giving her arm a twist,
But lately she's left me alone,
She doesn't follow me home.
Hopefully she's moved school, gone far away,
Now I'm not so scared about going to school every day.

Dulcie Parcell (11)

Football

I *like* football because it gets my pulse racing,
I run around the pitch kicking the golden ball.
I *love* football when I score a goal!
I hear the crowd calling my name, 'Sam,'
Which is the best sound of all!

I *hate* football when I miss a goal,
It makes me feel very small.
I *hate* football when the crowd shouts, 'Boo,'
As I want to run, run with the ball.

Sam Shone (11)

The Road

Tarnished with rosebuds, it hurries on.
We shout, running, gliding through the silky waves
And the swaying grasses.
Another bend.
Further forwards and laughter meets the broken gate
of stolen youth,
Where a butterfly strokes the bitter snow and a sunflower
tracks the path of the dying light through the haze.

Don't you remember?

Savage and tainted with frost, we march on, where icicles
grope the wintry stones and bare trees cradle the frozen ground.
Snaking on, its surface is a mirror of shattered glass:
blackened ice.
Yet no one slips beneath its darkened clutches – they cannot see,
but they know what waits in the sea of mist.
Or do they?
A façade of glittering beauty, a sea of wretched crystals,
A diamond ambush, it marches on.

I look behind, but can't turn back,
They've realised that
Not even you can run; spring into the road and face the hostile grip
of remorse.

Still it beckons us further.
Another step: another chime . . .
A moment lost.

Sasha Willmott (15)

True Colours

Pink

We were smitten
Cinema dates
Embarrassed smiles
Kisses on the doorstep

Red

We were dating
Afternoon strolls
Sweet fragrances
Roses left on the bed

Silver

We were engaged
A diamond ring
Champagne lunches
Weekends spent in Paris

White

We got married
A big white dress
Lots of presents
A gorgeous honeymoon

Grey

We were rowing
Hurtful insults
Slamming punches
Sleeping on the sofa

Blue

We had a fight
Paramedics
Flashing sirens
Intensive care visits

Black

We said goodbye
Bad memories
Tearful meetings
Signing divorce papers.

Jennifer Kay (14)

Do We Really Need War?

The main question is 'Who needs war?'
What is so important about having a war?
Why do countries have to bring up war in the first place?
If a country would care about all the people who die
They would forget about fighting straight away!
Think of all the innocent people who die,
All the people who are forced to join the army
Just because they are over the age of seventeen.
At the end of the day those who fight risk their lives.
Whichever country thinks they've won should be ashamed
Of themselves.
Many don't want war because after the war it's all loss,
As children have no parents, parents have no children,
Mothers are separated from their families,
Cities are shattered and ruined,
Lives are lost, people's homes have been burnt and destroyed.
Still the same question, 'Is war really necessary?'

Simran Bahra (12)

Friendship

Big people, small people
We have our own face
Stay together, play together
We're all a different race

Don't fight, don't fright
Keep the world in one place
Peaceful day, every day
We're all a different race

Love each other, hate each other
Don't be on the chase
Sunday, fun day
We're all a different race

Run fast, run slow
We have our own pace
Be a friend, be a friend
We're all a different race.

Suhail Ullah (11)

A Funeral

Speeches, laughter and sorrow
Tears, whimpers and cries
The thing that matters the most
Is the fact that we were here
To see him go.

The wooden coffin, six people held as
They slowly walked down the aisle
And placed it on the stand.

His spirit will lie within, although
His body will not
If they choose to be cremated
They will lie in ashes.

Neal Parker (11)

Dining Hall

The dining hall is loud
With screaming all around
Money rustling in pockets
As they try to get through the crowds

The teachers scream and shout
To get the children out
Because the bell's going to go
Any second now

There's burgers, chips and fries
In every single size
There's Coke and 7Up
That bring you a bit of luck

The dining room is closed
There's no more kids to go
The cleaners are all finished
And it's time to go home.

Ross Lee-Fowkes & Matty Boyes (11)

The Soldier

Shooting, shooting everywhere
Where they like, they just don't care

People dying, blood and gore
People sat on the floor

Soldiers laying in pools of blood
Soldiers hiding behind some wood

Corporal ordering soldiers about
Corporal shouting 'Out' and 'Out'

Tanks are trampling over the men
Soldiers hiding down in the den.

Scott Kilbride (12)

Red Is . . .

Red is my favourite football team.
Red is fire when a grand house is burning down very slowly.
Red is blood that keeps you going.
Red is love when you send someone a Valentine's.
Red is danger when my belly is hungry.
Red is anger when the other team score.
Red is shy when I get embarrassed.
Red is my favourite colour.
Red is ribbon on my cousin's doll.
Red is *stop!*

Joshua Vella (11)

All Around The World!

They're frightened, scared, alone,
They don't have a home.
All around the world!
A spoilt, greedy, sham,
They don't give a damn.
All around the world!
The happy, generous folk,
Their good spirits broke,
All around the world!

Rebecca Metcalf (11)

Red Is . . .

Red is anger when my parrot screams for attention
Red is anger when I get detention
Red is my favourite colour
Red is my secret lover
Red is the start of the rainbow
Red is the end.

Ashley Walker (11)

The Beach

Stretched out sleepily in the shade,
On a day when the sun's as fierce as a volcano.
I'm feeling so sticky and my face is as red as a plum,
The sea looks like lots of blueberries,
I head towards it for a swim
But the sand burns my feet like fire,
Making me run like air,
I'm so glad to reach the water.
I splash around like a dolphin,
The tiny waves welcome me like a bee attracted to a flower.

Jordan Fawcett (11)

Fire

Fire is red,
Fire is vicious,
It destroys everything in its path,
Fire is dangerous,
Fire, fire, fire.

Fire is destructive,
Fire is hot,
It burns when it touches,
Fire is afraid of water,
Fire, fire, fire.

Jordan Magee (11)

Happiness Is . . .

They smile at me,
I take a deep breath, it tastes nice,
I feel warm and snug,
It smells like sweets
And all I can do is laugh.

Kane Gough (11)

My Brother Tommy

When my brother Tommy
Sleeps in bed with me
He doubles up
And makes
Himself
Exactly
Like
A
V

And 'cause the bed is not so wide
A part of him is on my side.

Christopher Anderson (11)

Up Here

It's strange up here,
Not like down there,
Where the children snatch
And the people don't care.

Up here are the leaves,
Green, red and yellow,
Down there are the people,
Who scream and bellow.

For this is all I hear,
Every day and every night,
Because I am the giraffe,
Who has a very good sight.

Thomas Moore (12)

Winning Match!

Man Utd Vs Arsenal match 38
United need a point, are Arsenal too late?
The game kicks off, the crowd start to cheer
A first minute booking, the crowd start to jeer
Wenger and Ferguson shout out the tactics
Van Nistelrooy just misses with the acrobatics
The pace of the game builds up at speed
Both teams anxious to take the lead
Ljungberg to Pires, Wiltord to Cole
Cole through to Henry, a brilliant goal

Half-time whistle goes, Wenger shouts with glee
'If we keep playing like this, we can make it 3!'
In the other dressing room, the heads are down
Fergie screams and shouts and throws things around
Half-time subs made, Ronaldo's on for Scholes
Solskjaer is thrown on to bang in the goals
15 minutes in, Arsenal start to stray
They just can't afford to throw the points away
United clear a corner and start a counter attack
Campbell's still in the area, there's no centre back!

A cross comes in, Lehmann goes to get
He's missed completely, Keane bangs it in the net!
United are level, heads are up
United now favourite to take the cup!
It's almost over, the league's in sight
Man United look to have won the fight
One minute left, mistake by Cole
2-1, Giggs scores a brilliant goal!
Final whistle goes, the fans jump up
Man United have won the Premiership Cup!

Chris Himpleman (13)

I Thought I Was Great

I thought I was great
Much better than my mates

Then the shot went, I tripped over my lace
And fell on my face

Then I stood up and looked in front
Everyone was miles ahead

I ran and I ran
As fast as I could

Overtaking no one
As I thought I would

I am not so great
And I am not better than my mates.

Victoria Allard (12)

Martial Arts

M en and women both competing,
A renas packed full with supporters,
R eally nervous getting ready to fight,
T rying to get the gold,
I njuries galore,
A rm locks crippling opponents,
L eg locks doing the same.

A ll the attention is on the competitors,
R eferee watching over the match,
T rying to keep the score,
S ome people lose and others win.

Craig Coulam (13)

The Sloth

It is light grey
And it smells like fruit and daisies,
It has a long snout
And it is slow and lazy.

It climbs through the trees
With great ease,
Eating the leaves from the branches of the trees,
Until he gets attacked by bees!

Luke Colman (14)

Fear

Fear is black and tastes like evil,
It smells like dirt and grit,
It looks like darkness and sounds like screams
And also it feels *numb!*

When you overcome your fear,
You feel alive and free
And for those who haven't overcome their fear,
They should start to break *free!*

Daniel Benjafield (13)

Dolphins

D iving down to dangerous depths,
O cean currents swirling around,
L eaping high above boat decks,
P eople pointing as we frolic around,
H arpoon gun is pointed at us,
I n a panic we dart away,
N ow the spear soars . . . it misses!
S wimming quickly, off to play.

Katherine Thurlow (12)

Storm

It was a cold, rainy typical day
When the storm clouds came over our way
Black as darkness they sweep the land
God swipes the world with his big black hand

When the storm is over
And all the rain
Trickles down into the drain
And all the darkness has swept the land
God swipes others with his big black hand.

Todd Inns (14)

Cats

I spend my time on the prowl,
Listening to the toot of the owl,
Sniffing around for a snack,
Normally in the big black sack.
When I am happy, I love to purr,
When I wash, I lick my fur,
I love to have a sip of milk
And my fur feels as soft as silk.

Sam Morris (13)

Denise

D oes things to help others
E verything she does is fascinating
N ever sad
I nstead she is always happy
S he's beautiful
E very time she thinks, she's thinking of others.

Lee Williams (12)

See-Saw Haiku

See-saw like a boat
Slowly weighing both of you
Up and down it goes.

Amy Moss (12)

Birds Haiku

Birds flocked through the sky,
They all crashed onto the tree,
All screeching loudly.

Jonothon Griffen (12)

Hunting Earwig Haiku

A tiny earwig
Crawls through the midnight bushes
Looking for a home.

Leon Edmonds (12)

Moving Car Haiku

As the car roars by
Revving fiercely, very loud
Speeds away down road.

Sam Dunnett (12)

Surfing Haiku

He's up on his board,
Gliding through the crashing waves,
Wipe out on pipe line.

Louise Buck (12)

Graceful Swan Haiku

Gliding through the lake
Golden shining smooth feathers
The young glide behind.

Dominic Wood (12)

Moving Waves Haiku

Roaring sea hits boats
Broken pier smashes the waves
Ships making big swells.

Callum Parker (12)

Away From Home Haiku

An archway alone
Far from home living life rough
I've been pushed away.

David Harmer (13)

Having Moved Haiku

He moved from his home
Only finding a doorway
I wish someone cared.

Daniel Edney (13)

Moving Away Haiku

I feel upset, sad
Moved away from the hard pain
All I need is love.

Emma Clitheroe (13)

Moved Away Haiku

He has moved away
Only found a cardboard box
This man needs caring.

Brandon Westrup (13)

Moving Away Haiku

I am alone now
Cold and needing a warm bed
All I need is food.

Liam Wright (13)

The Sun

The sun is a roaring lion
Large and bright
Sitting there from day to night
Day by day the sun shines on him beneath
As the lion sits there chewing with his lethal teeth.

Corbin Griffen (12)

Funny

Funny is yellow
It tastes like chocolate and smells like sunflowers
Funny looks like the sun
It sounds like laughter and feels tickly.

Luke Thompson (12)

Moving Out To The Streets Haiku

All I need is love
Wanting only food and drink
I just need a friend.

Jenni Cockrill (13)

Moving Away Haiku

I see an old tramp
Homeless and cold in his box
No one to help him.

James Reeves (13)

Rapidity Gun

Swiftness is excellent, slowness is bad,
It's the most fantastic thing I've ever had,
You can go sluggish, you can go fast,
I've won every race in the past.

I'm the greatest athlete in a run,
That's why they call me Rapidity Gun,
They say when I run, I seem to fly,
That's why you see me frolic in the sky.

Oliver Marsden-Hill (12)

Up, Up And Away

There are many birds that fly,
That fly in the sky,
There are many birds that don't fly very high,
Some of them are birds of prey,
But the others were born a different way,
Some birds are very big and strong,
But the others are weak and long,
But there are many birds that don't fly,
Also others never see the sky.

Zack Sadler (12)

Feelings

Yellow is for happiness
When it is Saturday
But when Monday comes around
Red is for hate
Going to school for five days
Blue is for joy
For when Fridays are here.

Catherine Nobbs (12)

All About Nature

The fish swim in the sea
The waves crash over me

The water goes on for miles
Just like the sand goes on for miles

Some birds hover above the ground
While other birds like to sing and fly high above the ground

The long grass sways side to side
The air you cannot see, hides.

Jonathan Kirk (13)

Over The Meadows

The rattler slithers through the grass,
The elephant sways from side to side as I pass,
The eagle swoops and glides over the mountain high,
As the clouds float in the bright blue sky.

The monkeys swing from tree to tree,
The painted butterflies flutter gracefully,
Bees are zooming wild and free,
Over the meadows for all to see.

Alexander Stark (12)

Bird

I am a bird
I glide through the air
I flap my wings
With the wind
Whatever the time
Whatever the day
I will always be there in my cage.

Shelley King (12)

Bumblebee

It flies through the air so softly,
It won't hurt, don't stand away,
It collects pollen for honey,
Made in the hive all day.

So swift and quick it zooms,
It's as quiet as can be,
If you hear a buzzing sound,
It's a bumblebee.

It's black and yellow with wings,
It's stuck, it's trapped inside,
Let this buzzing creature go,
Let it out and let it survive.

So next time you spread honey on toast,
Just think, you see
That your delicious honey is made
By lots of bumblebees.

Philippa Shreeve (12)

Waves

Waves crashing on the shore,
Water rushing past to and fro,
Children playing in the water,
Running, jumping through the spray.

Speedboats moving through the water,
Skiers being dragged behind,
Seagulls flying overhead,
Swooping down for pieces of bread.

Sam Webb (12)

How Do You Feel?

How do you feel
When the sun shines bright?
Happy and glad
Like stars in the night,
Like a newborn lamb,
Like a picturesque sight,
How do you feel
When the sun shines bright?

How do you feel
When the thunderclouds boom?
Lonely and upset,
Like a forgotten room,
Like being on your own,
Like a flower that cannot bloom,
How do you feel
When the thunderclouds boom?

Georgia Donaldson (12)

Inside, Outside

Outside a monstrosity of a building
Inside an enormous piece of machinery with steaming funnels
Turning cogs
Conveyer belts leading into endless tunnels
Kilns making steam to fill the rooms like fog
Inside an enormous piece of machinery
Outside a monstrosity of a building

Inside an enormous piece of machinery
Outside a monstrosity of a building with a wide door
Massive car park
Wide enough to fit an army going to war
Made from a tarmac so dark
Outside a monstrosity of a building
Inside an enormous piece of machinery.

Mark Wyer (12)

My School Life!

The bell rings for lunch,
Children rushing everywhere,
Children run so fast,
An accident happens every time.

I sit on the wooden bench,
Longing heavily for a friend,
The school bullies take the mick,
Because I wear thick glasses.

'It's not my fault,'
I say to them,
They're not bothered,
As long as they have my money.

So every single week,
They get my two pounds,
Because I can't stick up for myself,
I always get pushed around.

The bell rings again,
It's time to go in,
They don't dare take the mick,
Because of Mr Jones.

So that's my school life,
I hate it so very much,
I'd just love to retire it,
But I can't you see!

Kelly Smith (12)

Tractor

The tractor trundles through the mud,
Braving saturated ground to sow the field,
Splattered with sloppy mud, caked in dirt,
The tractor trundles on,
Cheerfully does its job.

Jamie Childs (12)

The Storm

The thunder sat in a cloud,
The lightning struck churches and houses,
The sky was black with rage.

The thunder crashed down its heavy feet,
The lightning lashed out with its long arms,
The sky was white with fear.

The rain calmed the fires
As it poured from the sky,
Then everything was silent.

Leigh Rowland (13)

The Dragonfly

Dragonfly never stops moving
Red and green and coloured
He drifts up and down like a feather blowing in the wind
Gracefully flies high and low
Overflowing the skies
He buzzes a beautiful song
The great creature is tiny and speedy.

Ben Wynes (12)

Depression

Depression is a murky brown swamp,
It tastes like dirty water
And smells like rotting flesh,
Depression looks like a dull, dingy street lamp,
The sound of tears
And feels like complete emptiness.

Liam Howlett (13)

Sitting Round The Camp Fire

Sitting round the camp fire,
Ghost stories being told,
The crackling wood, the flames are hot
And keeps us from the cold.

Folk songs being sung,
As guitars quietly play,
Marshmallows being toasted
And talk of the good old days.

The flames are getting lower,
The night is closing in,
They're running out of songs
And the jokes are wearing thin.

Now the campers are tired,
It's time to end their day,
To their sleeping bags they snuggle
And the campfire fades away.

Aaron Critoph (12)

The Jaguar

Running is a special gift,
You're either born with it, or not,
But, if you're a jaguar,
It comes naturally,
Hunting, killing and is free,
Looking ready to go, even when still.

The streamlined body,
Takes off like it flies,
A speedy predator,
Pouncing like a coiled spring,
Catching its prey.

Sophie Dalgarno (12)

Dolphin

Swimming gracefully,
In the ocean waves.
Gliding silently,
On the water's surface.
Jumping happily,
Up into the sky.
Flipping perfectly,
Round through the air.
Splashing, clumsily,
Back into the sea.
Swimming swiftly,
Back
    Down,
        Down,
            Down,
                Into the murky deep.

Bethany Harris (12)

That House

I'll never forget that house
Shabby little windows
Stout little chimneys

That house made me feel
Joyful and happy
That house made me feel
Safe and sound

I would sit up late at night
In my rusty bed
And look up at its straw roof
Above my wondering head

Forever I have memories
Memories, memories, memories
Memories, memories.

Emma Crowther (13)

The Running Wind

Running down the street,
Against the running wind.
The wind is winning,
It's running, running,
As hard as it can.
The wind is huffed and puffed,
You fight back,
You reach the door,
You open it,
You've *won!*

Natasha Elby (12)

Night-Time

The night is so dark,
No light in the park,
Thousands of stars in the sky,
Children have been fed,
They're tucked up in bed
And there's not even a sigh.

Sarah Turner (12)

Ice

Ice is one big sheet of glass,
Cold like a freezer,
But melts when the sun shines down on it,
The rain falls slow, fast,
Wet like a full bath,
But dries up when the sun comes out.

Jason Fowler (12)

Depression

Depression is grey
It makes me feel capricious
Depression is grave
So damp and pale
Washed away like the rain
So wet
With tears in your eyes
Depressing's depressing, depressing, depressing
So when does it stop?

Jeff Carter (12)

Anger

Anger is dark red,
It tastes like cold carrot
And smells like a rotten body,
Anger looks like a cold, damp tunnel,
The sound of a train pounding on the tracks,
Anger sets your emotions high!

Shane Brinded (12)

Hate

Hate is dark red
It tastes like blood, warm in your mouth
Smelling like smoke leaking under a door
Hate spreads like fire
The clash of sword on sword
Hate terrifies me.

Iain Bean (12)

The Moods Of The World

Happiness makes you feel good,
Sadness makes you feel bad,
Joy makes you feel great,
Relief makes you feel glad.

Loneliness equals isolation,
Fun equals pleasure,
Boredom equals flatness,
But,
The truth is more than you can measure.

Thomas Gardiner (12)

Fear Is . . .

Fear is black like a witch's heart
Fear smells musky, rusty and dusty
Fear looks you straight in the eye
Fear makes you think you're going to die
Fear sounds oh so quiet
Fear in your mind is a manic riot
Fear searches your soul
And digs a deep hole.

Lewis Parr (12)

Cheetah

The cheetah zips out into the desert,
Searching for fresh meat for his evening feast,
He flashes around as quick as light,
Brightening up the murky night sky.

Adam Savoury (12)

A Turtle's Life

Out of the egg
Comes the baby turtle,
Forcing herself to the sand.
Over the grains
She clambers and struggles,
Looks back soulfully over the land.
She reaches the sea and paddles about,
With a flip of her flippers
And a sniff of her snout,
She swims away,
To the deep ocean blue,
Swimming away, away, away.
Round the world she travels,
Night and day,
Even though she sometimes loses her way.
Through warm tropical waters
And cold polar seas,
Circling every country, perfectly at ease.

Hannah Penney (12)

Sparrow

If I was a sparrow
I'd swoop through the cloudy sky
Cutting the air with my feathery wings
Greeting swallows, starlings, seagulls
I'd fly high
Then plunge back down to Earth
Open my wings to land
It's going to be bumpy . . .
Slowing down
Still . . .
I've landed.

Samantha Nudd (13)

A Bee's Life

Fluffy bee buzzes past,
Flying through the tall flowers,
Picks a flower and drinks the nectar,
Chooses another and another.

Busy bee cannot stop,
For he will almost never drop,
Busy bee can't you see,
You need to find another bee!

Bzzzzzz, bzzzzzz, bzzzzz.

Flies into an open window,
Zooms through the television,
Sits on top of a yellowish fruit,
Then flies away as an object shoots.

Again, he sits down onto a table,
Another object crashed down.

The bee is no more,
That's for sure!

Yasmin Pattrick (12)

School

School is bad,
School is good,
School is sad,
School is fruit,
School is where you go to learn,
School is where your reputation turns,
School is funny,
School is fearful,
School is where you can see your future clearly,
I like school.

Craig Bone (12)

Darkness

Silent and swift,
Creeping up,
Through the mist,
It wanders past,
Spreading near and far,
Bringing out the smallest star.
It sneaks up,
On innocent homes,
Never stops,
Always roams,
Feet tired,
But on it goes,
Where it's going,
No one knows,
The darkness.

Stacey Sanderson (13)

Fear

Fear is a veteran warrior
Swift and sudden
It strikes
With its killing blow

Fear is a bulbous maggot
On and on it eats
Away
With its miniscule teeth

Fear is a ruthless bacteria
Multiplying by thousands every second
Until it overcomes you
Slowly wiping you out.

Raleigh Jenner-Hillard (12)

Love

Love is bright red
It tastes like warm apple pie
Love smells like newly-mown grass
It looks like a garden full of big red roses
The sound of wedding bells in the distance
Love feels happy and peaceful.

Rebecca Quinn (13)

Fire

Flames from the bonfire twist and turn in the cold air
Smoke from the bonfire rushes out through the sky
Logs in the bonfire dissolve into the sizzling fire
Ashes from the bonfire float around the black sky
Heat from the bonfire pours out like lava.

Joshua Hannon (12)

Time

The rhythmic ticking clock marks the passage of time,
Counting down the minutes till the end of the line,
Moving very slowly in our carefree childhood days,
Moving ever faster as life ebbs away.

Serena Pattrick (14)

Anger

Anger is bright metallic red
It tastes like blood and bones
Anger is the smell of jealousy and sweat
It sounds like bells and loud music.

Daniel Robbins (12)

Classroom

Pens, pencils, paper,
Children running round and round,
Oh what a clatter!
That screeching sound
Of the chalk on the blackboard,
The teacher saying to a child,
'Oh, what's the matter?'
Lazy children daydreaming,
The teacher's voice drifting away,
Children screaming,
Teachers shouting, chairs scratching along the floor,
Then *ring*, the children run out,
Classroom deserted!

Sophie Coomer (12)

The Plane

Old rusty plane,
Soaring through the sky,
Streamlined as a pie,
Twist, twirl, loop, dive,
Engine stuttering, stalling and sloping,
Crashing down to the Earth.

Brendan Johnson (13)

Sunset

The sun sets
As the night falls
Stars come out in the sky
The moon falls asleep
A dog howls.

Kelly Sims (12)

Tripping Out!

I like packing for a trip
Anticipation, readiness to begin
Sitting by water
Sun so bright, the black ink looks red
Calm now – to remember later
In less still moments
Carry it forward to still my anxious heart
Not quite ready to move
But the muscles are remembering
Action
Twitching, aches, ready to sprint
Zinnias in vase dying
Summer is going
Changes are beginning

When the movement has ended
Wonders how I got here
To this place
Not very far from any place else
Just tiny movement
In my head, in time
Away from you
Confusion at missing you
But not
Two days before here
It was the same old
But in four hours
It changes
I don't think you'll understand where I've gone
Without you.

Hannah Baker (13)

In The Cage

Every day the same old view,
Every day the same old space,
Every day children pointing,
Every day pointing and laughing,
Every day the same old view, over again,
Every day the same old food,
Every day the same old schedule,
Every day I climb up metal bars,
What am I?
I am a monkey in a metal cage!

Mark Webster (13)

Depression

Depression is grey,
It tastes like cold rotten fish
And smells like a musky, wet blanket,
The sound of an echoing cry,
Depression,
Depression intimidates me.

Natasha Parramint (12)

Weather Happiness

I love letting my toes wiggle around in the wild breezy sea,
When I'm running the hot stuffy air takes my breath out of me.
The wind comes at me like it is a fierce piece of writing printed in bold,
I love it when down comes the warm sunbeams
Because at night-time it gives me nice dreams.
All in all, I feel that the weather makes me happy in all sorts of ways,
Even if do have stormy, rainy days!

Stacey Cummings (12)

The Movement Of The World

When I was a child
I saw things move,
People like me walking,
Cars move just like trolleys,
Robots and factories move,
But in a different sort of way,
Trees sway from side to side,
Green grass rustles when people tread on it.

Wind, sun and moon all come and go,
Oh and the rain!
Aeroplanes, lorries, cars, buses all move,
Some fly like the wind,
Some move like the sun and moon,
Everything moves because
We move it!

Daniela Balls (13)

Rabbits

My rabbit's name is Badger,
His teeth are as sharp as knives,
He loves to eat the plants,
He crunches carrots constantly,
His twitching nose always brings him to food,
His ears are big and fluffy, good for hearing,
His tail is like a lump of cotton wool,
He is as white as snow,
He moves very fast like a train,
He thinks he's a dog when he chases cats,
When the sun is blazing hot he loves to sunbathe,
He loves his new hutch, it's red, blue and yellow,
He makes me very happy and we all love him.

Louise Waplington (13)

I'm So Lonely

Sitting here on my bed underneath my sheet,
I feel like I am going to weep; I cannot sleep,
I am so lonely, please help me,
I feel like someone is trying to clone me.

The wind is whistling through the crack in the wall
And the trees are tapping on the window like someone's call,
I am so lonely, I feel as if someone is trying to get through to me.

I am getting so scared, because I am not prepared
For what may lie ahead in life,
I have a pipe, I play it loud so I cannot hear the racket outside,
I am so lonely, please help me decide where to lead my life.

I am getting hot, I cannot breath
And the tension in the room is too much for me, don't you see,
Don't you see, I am so lonely please help me.

I am so lonely, I am so lonely,
Please show me the way to go.

Emma Fraser (12)

My Cat . . .

My cat called Tigger, moves in all different ways,
She stretches like a giraffe's neck, thin and very long.
She is all different colours, black, brown and white,
She sprawls out, she is like a white rabbit,
Because she is fluffy and cute,
She is long and furry,
She leaps like Tigger out of Winnie the Pooh,
She crawls like a spider,
She has lots of energy like a cheetah,
She is my cat, Tigger, we love her very much.

Katie Johnson (13)

Football

Nerves rattle the player's body,
As he steps up for the free kick.

Blood rushing to his head,
He must concentrate, he must score.

He steps up positioning himself for a left foot stroke,
He can feel the adrenalin rush right through him.

Legs trembling like they had turned to jelly.

The player looks confident,
The keeper does not.

The player strikes forward, wind rushing through his hair,
Then striking the ball.

The ball rises and rises,
It spins like a comet soaring through the air.

The keeper makes his move,
Plunging forwards, towards the post.

The keeper is close,
However it cruelly curled away from the keeper.

Bang! Top corner strike,
Goal, the crowd roar frantically in applause.

The player bows,
He scored because he believed in the ball.

Own the ball and you will own the game.

Lewis Hall (12)

The Person Who Never Was

Every day I wonder how did it all slip away?
I'm sitting at home desperate to know why!
Sitting through my agonising torture,
As I'm dressed in my smart uniform,
Ready to walk to school,
I always stop on the way,
Getting into a delirious state,
I feel such contempt for this person,
I want to fall prostrate to slumber on the ground beneath me,
But an instinct inside me is holding me up,
Maybe it's the person,
Or maybe it's the sheer treacherous behaviour of myself,
I've got to admit sometimes I have violent behaviour,
But I never mean it,
Whoever or whatever this person was,
They are very timely,
But it never was,
It was the person that never was . . .

Adam Baisley (13)

My Motion Poem

Movement is a marvellous thing,
It makes you want to leap and sing,
It lets you walk, it lets you prance,
It lets you run, it lets you dance,
It lets you jump, it lets you skip,
It even lets you do a flip!
Yes, movement is a marvellous thing,
It makes you want to leap and sing.

Sam Durrant (12)

Tired Motion

It is the last lesson of the day,
I slump down in my chair in a very tired way,
I pull out my school books from my bag and drop them on my desk,
The teacher sets some writing work, but we really want to rest,
I see tired motion all around!
When people's pens fall on the ground,
They're picked up very slowly but they never seem to write at all,
Every movement seems so very small,
Except from the teacher writing, his hand moving rapidly,
But we all can't wait until it's a Saturday,
At last the sound of the bell bounces off the walls,
'Quick, pack up!' the teacher calls,
Now the tired motion has changed as children sprint out of class
Like a charging stampede,
As tired motion has turned into speed!

Luke Rushbrook (12)

Autumn

Leaves falling day by day,
Autumn is not far away,
Leaves coloured orange, yellow, red,
All the woods now one leaf bed.

It is cold outside, but inside is warm,
Put your fire on to keep away the storm.
The cosy fire which keeps you warm at night,
Don't let the lightning give you a fright.

Because in the morning, it will be alright,
First look at the amazing sight.

Jason Snowling (12)

Cycling To School

I reluctantly wake,
Open the curtains,
Chill breaks in,
Slog downstairs,
Quick breakfast,
Open the back door,
See the bike,
Shimmering in the rain,
Get on the saddle,
Pedals turning,
Handlebars frosted,
Gears changing,
Arrive at lights,
Fingers numb,
Feet freezing,
Dismount and sigh,
Lock up with relief.

Adam Smith (12)

Shop!

Shop, shop, shop!
Shop until you drop!
Shop until you've got everything,
Shop, shop, shop!

Shop, shop, shop!
Shop with your mates.
Shop with your family,
Shop, shop, shop!

Shop, shop, shop!
Shop for fun!
Shop because you have to!
Shop, shop, shop!

Sophie Brown (12)

Movement Comes

Movement comes from . . .
I would have to say . . .
Boredom and
The hate of rain

Movement comes from . . .
I would have to say . . .
Wishing away the day
Fighting nature's ways

Movement comes from . . .
I would have to say . . .
Riding Harleys
The American way

Movement comes from . . .
I would have to say . . .
Bombing
Saddam Hussein

Movement comes from . . .
I would have to say . . .
Drinking my
Pepsi cola
Every day

Movement comes from . . .
I would have to say . . .
With United
Winning the
Premiership
Again.

Wayne Diggines (13)

Dad's New Car!

I got up extra early today,
Dad's getting a new car!
He's giving me a ride in it,
I hope we're going far!

When we arrive back home,
We're giving it a clean,
He says he wants to see my face
And he wants the car to gleam!

After cleaning we are topping her up,
In petrol I mean,
Dad says I can fill her up,
So our car'll be topped up and clean!

Then we have to make sure
She has water in her tank,
That is so she can clean her windows,
But for now we are off to the bank!

Lisa Roberts (12)

Poetry In Motion

He was focusing right to the end,
Then it came to the end.
It just didn't feel right,
He flew through the air as though he was light.
The grass stains on his knees,
It felt as though he'd been stung by a thousand bees.
He got back up,
Like a young pup,
Grass stains glowing,
He kept on going.
He got to the end,
He thought it was a shame about that bend.

Ryan Edmonds (12)

My Poem In Motion

I'm travelling to London
I'm now on the M25
We've been in the car for ages
And so many have passed by

I can't wait to get out of the car
It's so stuffy and hot
I can't stand long journeys
As my head hurts a lot

'Are we there yet? Are we there yet?'
That's all my sister keeps saying
My mother is asleep
Even though the music is playing

We soon arrive at London
Lots to see and lots to do
I've been on the London Eye
And gone to London Zoo

It feels as if we've just arrived
But we are already packed
Returning home to Yarmouth
I can't wait till we come back!

Remy Browning (13)

Shark

There's a shark in the water swimming around,
You can't see or hear a sound,
It's a shark, oh no, he's heading this way
He's heading fast, towards the bay.

You'd better get out of the water, quick,
The shark's coming to take his pick.
The swimmers quickly swim to the beach,
Completely out of the shark's reach.

Nicola Leggett (13)

Poetry In Motion

As I paddle in the clear blue sea,
Gazing across the horizon,
A far out boat, the size of a pea,
The sun, slowly rising.

The cool wind blowing through my hair,
The fluffy clouds up in the sky,
Breathing in the clean, fresh air,
The bright rays from the sun, shining in my eye.

Looking through my sunglasses,
Makes everything much darker,
Even as the sun passes,
It looks like someone has gone over everything
With a big black marker.

Playing with my bucket and spade,
In the golden sands,
Admiring what others have made,
Including prints of their hands.

As I paddle in the clear blue sea,
Watching the children netting,
A far out boat, the size of a pea,
The sun slowly setting.

Victoria Lucas (12)

Butterfly

I saw it flying in the sky
But it never ever went that high
Its wings would flutter all the time
It never flew in a straight line
But it was such a lovely butterfly!

Emma Huggins (12)

Rivers Run

Rivers run to place to place,
When they are together they are one face.
It moves like a person when he walks,
But the only thing that the river can't do is talk.

When the river travels to the ocean,
The river dreams of his emotion.
When the river tries to climb the waterfall,
The river just rushes down as a fool.

River is together and forever rowing,
Travelling, endlessly flowing,
The river finally ends flowing
And newborn rivers to continue rowing,
Where it pleases and continually gushing,
To place to place rushing.

Kyran Smith (13)

The Sun

I'm a flame and a fire
I'm a blaze and your desire
I'm a running down the street
Ya can't a catch me, I'm a treat
I'm a breeze now a cooling
I'm all over for another forty
As I come, people a yawning
But as I go people a snoring
Ready for morning
Morning
Morning.

Andrew Wells (13)

Friends On The Move

We were good friends,
Who would be there for each other
And stand up for each other,
Until the end.

We grew up together,
Went to school with each other.

When you got married, I was there for you,
When you got married, I was there for you too.
You had a baby girl, I had two boys,
Who played together with all of their toys.

Then came the day,
In the middle of May,
With sorrow you had to say,
You and your family were moving away.

I knew you had to go to the city,
But my heart was full of pity.
I miss you very much,
But we vowed to keep in touch.

We grew up together,
Went to school with each other.
Now those memories,
Will stick with us forever.

Kayleigh Hickey (13)

The Snake

He slips, he slides, all day and all night
He hides, he crawls and gives you a fright
He hunts in the day
And then at night
He coils up and sleeps tight.

Jade-Karly Hurrell (13)

The Par Five Hole

The green is so far away,
I try to get there in one massive shot,
But I find that it went terribly awry,
As the ball travels as far as if I had not.

I try to play a really good shot,
But that ball's a really good jumper,
I think my golf's going to pot,
'Cause the ball hopped into a bunker!

After a big chip shot out of the trap,
I manage to get on the green,
I go to fetch my putter
And put the ball out of the scene.

I don't think I should play anymore,
Because I couldn't hit it far,
Though I'll keep my handicap 34,
'Cause I still got it under par!

Samuel Reynolds (13)

A Football Match

The ball is spinning
The team is picked
The goalkeeper is grinning
The ball is kicked

The crowd cheering and jumping
The goal nets swaying
Players' adrenaline pumping
The players are playing

The striker scores
It's now two-one
There is a great applause
My team has won!

Sam Alden (12)

Locomotion

Train, thundering, clickety, clack,
Speeding down the railway track.
Whistle blowing, tunnel in sight,
Single ghostly night light.

A sigh, a *whoosh*, it passes on,
Intercity, four carriages long.
Passengers await their time,
For the end of the line.

Bradley Vlachos (13)

Fox Hunt

Running from its predator,
Running for its life.
Running with a cub in her mouth,
Afraid of the hunter's knife.

With panic in her eyes,
As she runs through the wood,
Chased by the hounds,
Would they hurt her, yes they would!

Stephanie McKnight (12)

The Waves, Tide And Sea

When the waves come to shore
The sand it does look so poor
And when the tide goes in
I have nothing but sin
That's when I sleep
I only weep
That someday the waves will hurt me
When I'm by the sea.

Matthew Anniss (12)

Mother Nature's Wish

Ants and bats, pigs and rats,
Horses, cows and frogs,
Growling lions in the grass,
Howling wolves and dogs.

Slithering snakes, quiet and slick,
Slow, prickly hedgehogs,
A spider monkey in a tree,
Millipedes on logs.

Tiny little ants,
Scurrying up the trees,
Bouncing kangaroos,
Clouds of dust they leave.

Giant wrinkly elephants,
Squirting water high,
Birds are flying all around,
Trying to keep dry.

Quick and slender tigers,
Are hunting down their prey,
Her cubs are waiting eagerly,
For what they'll eat today.

Yellow ducks and ducklings,
Multicoloured fish,
Buzzing bees around the flowers,
Mother Nature's wish.

Lucy Burns (12)

Motion

Motion is something we can't live without,
What would we do if we couldn't move about?
What would we do if we couldn't sing and dance
And what would we do if we couldn't jump and prance?

Movement is something we can't live without,
If we all couldn't move we would all scream and shout.
What would we do if we couldn't stretch and bend?
We wouldn't be able to run to a friend.

Motion is something we can't live without,
What would we do if we couldn't move about?
What would we do if we couldn't run a race
Or even just walk at our own special pace?

Amy Tovell (12)

A Morning At The Beach

At dawn I jumped out of bed
Ready for my morning trip
Grabbing my little friend's leash
Thanking me, she gave me a lick

I opened the door, she dashed out
She knew we were going away
My canine friend by my side
Until at the beach we play

The sounds of waves filled our ears
As we played catch in the sand
How we love our morning trips
The beach is a peaceful land!

Kayleigh O'Connor (12)

Water

Water twists and turns round bends,
It crashes up the banks,
Gushing over waterfalls
And making masses of waves.

Further down the stream,
The water is clear
And fish swim with speed,
While it trickles over rocks.

Speeding out to sea,
The current gets quicker;
The waves become greater
And the crashes sound like thunder.

Dolphins jump in and out of the sea,
Making splashes as they dive back in.
The water bubbles and froths,
As the waves crash onto the beach.

Katherine Taylor (14)

Poetry In Motion!

She walks along, scuffing her small brown shoes
Along the dusty, deserted street.
She moves slower than a snail,
Sometimes lifting her heavy head to gaze at the empty sky.
No bees hum or birds tweet,
So she drops her head to see her feet.

No movement, no sound or existing life,
Her dreams, her nightmares about her strife.
Years have past since she had a friend,
No Christmas, no Easter, no summer or spring,

She sits in a corner and wishes her life away,
Maybe she'll find someone and be happy again.

Rebecca Rigby (12)

Getting Lost At Sea

The boat rocks gently,
A cold breeze in my face,
The sun shining in the sky,
What a beautiful day.

Suddenly the sky turns black,
The wind gets faster and faster,
Heavy rain starts to fall,
A storm is brewing.

The lightning crashes down,
As its rays fill the sky
And the rain keeps on pouring,
Getting heavier and heavier.

The sound of the thunder
And the howling wind, keep
Rocking the boat more and more,
Until eventually it can't take it anymore.

Bang! The boat goes as it tips over,
Crashing on the waves,
I get taken out to sea,
Will I ever get home?

Laura Inal (12)

Rally

Car numbers on the door
The cars really fly
Pedals to the floor
Spoilers hung high
The cars really motor
Especially the Toyota
Tracks curved and straight
Colin McRae is so great.

Andrew Hemp (12)

Him

Standing on the bridge I hear
Frantic cries, my father's shouts
I block them

This night is for only one thing
I think as the river churns below
The tears flow

I think of good times and of bad
His smile, his eyes and his love
And I listen

The day he went was horrifying
Talking, a car, a screech of brakes
And a scream

The wind howls around me
And dares me to jump but I hear him
I hear him

'Come down,' he calls and calls again
His spirit surrounds me
And I feel him

He stretches out his hand to me
I turn around and I obey
And he's gone.

Jessye King (12)

Grounded

Looking through the window,
In my bedroom,
I look outside
And feel the gloom,
Children playing,
Laughter sounded,
I can't go out 'cause I am grounded!

Sam Gilham (12)

Water's Alive

Early in the morning the water awakes
Followed by the whale and the howling it makes
The dolphins jump and fill the skies
And the fish start swimming as they fly

The water's moving, it's really alive
The dolphins swim in groups of five
As the water flows like you've never seen
Under it lies fish playing mean

The sky's dark and the stars are out
Everyone looks including the trout
The fish go to bed and turn out their lights
They all do this as they say goodnight.

Zoe Knell (12)

Clouds

There once was a cloud floating by,
Way, way up in the sky.
It looked like a cat
And then like a bat,
Which then flew way, way up high.

This little cloud floated down
And turned itself into a clown.
Which then I can say
It did float away,
Yes, floated away round the town.

Francesca Watts (13)

Why?

Why does the sun shine,
the rain fall,
the snow lay?

Why do people cry,
people laugh
and people sigh?

Why are there feelings
like love, hate
and jealousy?

Why is there birth,
life
and death?

Why is there pain,
so sore
and so tender?

Why?

Lauren Skoyles (12)

The Dolphin

Jumping and gliding as it slickly moves through the waves,
Still on its journey as the sunset fades.
Making watery splashes,
As it dives and dashes.
Singing its song.
As it swiftly moves on.

Beneath the waves,
Where it dives and braves.
The dangers of the sea,
As it swims to be free.

Bethany Fuller (12)

My Brother

My brother is small and slim
He has a cheeky grin
He keeps the TV all day
And I have to go and play

My brother's a bit of a pain
But he hates it when it rains
He gets rather bored
When he can't go on his skateboard

My brother has lots of mates
And goes out on a lot of dates
He can't wait to get out of school
'Cause he wants to go and play pool

My brother acts cool
When he plays football
He likes sports
And all sorts
But on top of that, he's my brother.

Danielle Emons (12)

Cars On A Motorway

Standing on a bridge,
Over the motorway,
Watching cars
Zooming past
At 70mph.

There are so many cars,
Lorries big and small cars,
But the best car I have seen
Is the silver Mercedes Benz,
With a silver shining beam.

Jamie Lack (12)

Alternating Weather

Pouncing like a cat
Growling like a dog
The rain is falling down
There's thunder and there's fog

Clouds roll and race away
Sprinting like a girl
The sun is coming up
It's as gorgeous as a pearl.

Daniel Snowling (12)

The Cheetah

The cheetah's legs fly through the air,
He has black spots all over his hair,
In a flash of light,
He's out of sight.

He stalks his prey with stealth and wits
And then he rips it to little bits,
He's too fast to see,
He could be round you or me.

Joe Payne (12)

Dolphins

D elicately they move through the waters,
O ver the crashing waves,
L ike horses jumping over a steeple.
P eople watch in amazement on how they jump so high,
H ow I wish to be like them,
I n the clear blue seas.
N o fears or worries to problem them, as they keep on,
S ailing by and by.

Georgia Lewis (12)

Death

With all the dead folk of this land
We should never just wait and stand
Men, women and young children too
One day death will swallow you
We are dead, our corpses stink
We are here to make you think
When you're dead, your bodies rot
All your things are worth not a lot
Only good deeds will save your soul
When you fall in death's big dark hole.

Luke Dougan (13)

Two Minutes To Live!

I plunge into darkness,
Silent whispers whirl around me,
I'm spellbound in this hell.
Won't somebody relieve me of this intense place?
My vision appears smudged
And my voice leaks out as an echo,
I sprint as fast as I can but time has slowed me down,
I reach for my clock but the time has run out!

Jade Dobner (13)

Poetry In Motion

Flying,
Higher than the wind.
Soaring,
So close to the sun.
Feeling,
Freer than the air.
Nobility and dignity in one.

Matthew Sharp (14)

Running Water

Water runs from a tap,
Trickles along through every gap.
Choppy, calm, shallow and deep,
Running down your face when you weep.

Rivers start as a shallow pool,
Up high in the mountains where it is cool.
The gorge is next in line,
With the mountain valley steep sides.

Now it meanders to and fro,
While tributaries join the main river flow.
As we come to the end and the mouth,
It finds that the sea is in its path.

Samantha Noble (13)

Poetry In Motion

When I think of motion,
I think of a car,
Speeding down the road,
Travelling quite far.

When I think of motion,
I think of a train,
Clicking on the rail tracks,
Even in the rain.

When I think of motion,
I think of my mum,
Always running after me,
Until the job is done.

Tiffany Sargeant (13)

Never Still

Emotions are hidden feelings
Like a trapped soul longing to escape,
As the hours, days, weeks, months and years pass,
The crying and screams of hurt,
Slowly turn to happy smiling faces.

But too quickly emotions change like the speed of lightning,
Transforming a beautiful figure,
To a burning nightmare,
In a speeding second.

Happiness cries fleetingly with joy,
As the welcoming feeling of love surrounds you,
Like a warm cover encircling you with timeless love.

Second by second, day by day,
Our emotions change,
Like the ticking of a clock
And the motion of time . . .
Never still.

Ellis King (14)

The Man's Son

The man liked his son's football
But it was quite shocking
He was a dirty player
So he got a booking

He was sent off
But he didn't think it was right
He went to the changing room with a fright
He tried to get through a gap but it was too tight

Full-time was in nine
The players were good
But man of the match was mine.

Charlie Chesney (12)

The Race

The race began,
John was in the lead,
He tripped over a can,
He was last.

His knee was bleeding,
But he didn't care,
He was gaining,
He was fifth.

He kept on running,
He was fourth,
His knee kept on bleeding,
But he didn't care.

He was third,
He wanted to win,
He stepped on a dead bird,
But he kept on running.

He was second to the lead,
He wanted to win,
He was gaining speed,
He was like a lean mean running machine.

He was first,
The end was in sight,
His lungs felt like they were going to burst,
He won the race and everybody cheered.

Joseph Drewery (12)

Time

You can forget it
You can know it
You can feel it
You can see it

The animals know it
The planets adjust to it
The trees have rings because of it
The tides turn to it

You can't reverse it
You can't alter it
You can't make it
You can't be it

The rocks can't stop it
The sky turns dark because of it
The world lives it
And we are gone to it . . .

Time . . .

Hadyn Everson (13)

Tiger

Tiger, tiger
Orange and bright,
Tiger, tiger
Do you hunt at night?

Tiger, tiger
Bright and bold,
Tiger, tiger
No more needs to be told.

Nikita Staff (12)

The Wheel Of Water

New life for a stream,
Born in the mountains,
Having fun in the snow,
Stopping in the frost.

Gushing, rushing, precipitation,
Pushing down a steep edge,
Powering turbines as it goes,
Wearing away the banks.

Farmers drinking water – irrigation,
Crops towering and tasty,
Feeding many open mouths,
What will we do without water?

For a river, a town is a rubbish tip,
Rivers choke, garbage swells in their maw,
The energy from the childhood has gone,
But still the river pushes on.

At last the sea, the river is free,
Frolicking with the waves,
Interrupted whilst basking in the sun,
It's swept up, away then parted.

Constructing cumulus clouds,
That drift high above,
Precious droplets like eggs,
On touchdown they're born.

New life for a stream,
Born in the mountains,
Having fun in the snow,
Stopping in the frost . . .

Jennifer Durrant (13)

Going Up A Hill

Going up a hill
On my little bike
Going up the hill in fright
Pushing my feet up right up to my limit
As hard as I can
Nearly dodging a van
Nearly at the top, running out of air when suddenly
I didn't care
For I was there
Right at the top of the hill
So pleased with myself I didn't notice
That I was falling down the hill
I was so scared
That I thought I was dead
So I closed my eyes in dread
To find out I was in bed dreaming one of my nightmares again.

Liam Applegate (12)

Black Beauty!

They run swift as the blowing winds,
Racing the eagles through valleys and streams,
Their beautiful long tails streaming behind,
Like multicoloured banners,
Many hooves beating the ground,
Give the sound of distant thunder echoing on,
Then quiet while grazing, still and at peace,
Beautiful colours, golden, chestnut and brown,
Foals gently nursing from their dams,
The stallion forever watchful protecting,
Handsome and proud,
But turning to pure fury,
He protects his herd!

Shauna Reid (13)

The Stream Of Four Seasons

It starts off in spring,
As a tiny little source,
A trickle from a mountainside,
Chasing the wind as it goes.

Now it is summer,
It is slowly becoming a river,
It meanders through bends
And gushes through valleys.

Autumn is now falling,
Leaves are swallowed by the river.
Tributaries are joining,
It rapidly makes its way.

Winter has come round again,
Ice is slowly freezing the river,
It is getting engulfed,
It struggles to reach its destination.

Spring has appeared once more,
The ice is breaking.
The river reaches the sea
And somewhere up another mountain a source is being born.

Mandy Mullender (13)

Lone Wolf . . .

Creeping through the thickest snow in the dead of night,
Watching prey near and by for his time to strike,
Prowling around the towering trees, playing in the autumn leaves,
Padding along in a coat of grey, under the coolest trees he lies,
Teeth so sharp they bite through bone,
Through the landscape he will forever roam,
No place will truly be his home, destined to walk this Earth alone.

Jamesina Buchan (14)

Living

People are happy and sad,
Animals fierce and friendly.
Dogs bark,
Babies cry,
All over the enormous round world.

The sky is blue as the ocean,
The sand as golden as glitter.
People jump, jump and jump,
On the big, bold beach.

The desert is hot and dry,
The Atlantic is icy and cold,
Wolves howl,
Fish freeze,
All over the enormous round world.

Rachel Ballanger (12)

A Living Shadow

A shadow is a person,
Wandering around in its own world,
Nothing can stand in its way,
Up the walls and along the floor,
It looks like it is trying to escape.

Wherever you go, whatever you do,
You will never be alone.
When you look over your shoulder,
Your shadow will follow not too far behind,
It can feel a bit creepy,
But you know you are never alone.

Cathy Robertson (13)

Bella

Her name is Bella,
She's not very energetic,
She is so lazy.

Bell is only three,
I call her Bell just for short,
She is a blue roan.

I love my horse, Bell,
We have bonded together,
She is really fab.

It's near winter now,
She has to be all rugged up,
'Cause she'll get a cold.

Bella eats all day,
Carrots, apples and polos,
My horse is healthy!

Leigh Rogers (13)

The Spider

Scurry, scurry the spider runs
Over the walls and trees
Legs hit the ground one by one
Creeping through grass and leaves

Quickly the spider weaves his web
In a gap quite long and narrow
Then when the fly lands on the web
He strikes just like an arrow

Slipping, sliding, the spider tries
To escape the shiny sink
Then quite exhausted, there he lies
Before he's washed away in a blink.

Joe Stringer (12)

The Race

The start man said, 'Go'
My heart was beating
I drove quite slow
I wish I was teaching

I went round the course
Turning left and right
I twisted the throttle
And held on real tight

I passed the first
And started to try
Then hitting a bump
I started to fly

I turned the bend
And up the jump
I saw the end
And landed with a clump

I went past the line
I was in first place
The trophy was mine
I could see it shine.

Dean Borley (12)

The Wind

The wind howls,
Like a wolf ready for the hunt.
It preys upon the trees,
Stealing his leaves.
With his fearsome cry,
People stand by,
Watching as the wind,
Fails to give in.

Natasha Fenn (13)

Creatures Come Out At Night

As the drained sun sets
And the people fall asleep,
The houses sit in silence,
Until the creatures creep . . .

. . . They crawl up the plugholes
And slide down the walls,
Round the newly infected curtains
And across the naked floors.

They glare at your unsettled stirring
In your bed,
Watching, listening and wandering
Above and below your head.

But when the sun rises,
That's when they know,
They better tiptoe home,
Until the sun once again hangs low . . .

Staci Barnes (14)

Cars

Cars go fast,
Cars go slow,
When you're 17 you can have a go.

Red and yellow, blue and green,
Every colour you have seen.

When the engines roar,
See them soar.

Sports cars go vroom,
Banger cars go boom.

Akita Greenwood (12)

Tuscan TVR

I lay in bed at night and dream,
Of joining the Le Mans team,
Driving a TVR, my favourite car,
24 hours to see how far.

200 miles down the Mulsanne straight,
Listen to the roar of that big V8,
Lights that twinkle in the dark,
Listen to that exhaust bark.

Tyres are worn, fuel is low,
Into the pits and off we go,
The sun is up, end of the race,
My TVR is in first place.

Remove the dirt, time for a clean,
Tuscan TVR,
What a beautiful machine.

Craig Hockton (13)

Old Cat

It purrs like the wind
And the claws are sharp daggers,
Their eyes beamed at the sun,
Its twirling, twizzling tail,
The sour hearing of the sweet noise,
The body is like a velvet balloon,
Its legs are binding twigs
And its nose sniffs out the birds,
Its weary, wavy whiskers,
The gentle tiptoeing on the delicate grass.

Jade Inns (13)

The Deadly World Of Transport

The deadly world of transport,
Rushing down the road,
Not taking any notice,
Of the Highway Code.

Crashes always happen,
On the train track,
Tears on people's faces,
Not looking back.

Not all planes are problem free,
Troubles may occur,
A metal heap on the ground,
The rest is all a blur.

The deadly world of transport,
Rushing down the road,
Not taking any notice
Of the Highway Code.

Natalie Routledge (12)

My Mum

My heart tingles
Whenever I hear your name
You are the best mum
Everyone should think the same
When I am ill you stand by me
I can tell you my secrets
And you help me to be what I want to be
You are the coolest
I admire what you do
I love my mum
And so should you.

Sophie Baker (13)

My Garden

The sun shone down
On the morning dew
The steam rose up
Into the sky so blue

The flowers swayed
In the light breeze
Moving from side to side
With such ease

The insects awoke
From their sleep
To climb the stalks
Which stood so steep

The birds chirped as
The morning came
They sang his tune
And all sounded the same

The old lady walked
To the gate
To look for the postman
Who was running late

The dog ran out
Across the lawn
While the old lady
Took a yawn.

Elliot Fuller (12)

The Motion Of The Car

Shiny,
Smooth,
Sleek and
Streamlined,
Wheels rotation,
Metal clanging,
Engines roaring,
Mass of metal,
Windows reflecting,
Gliding smoothly,
Noise of children
From within,
Shiny,
Smooth,
Sleek and
Streamlined.

Lorraine Bell (13)

The Master Of The Night

He swoops and hovers
On wings so light,
He's known as the master
Of the night.

With eyes that see
Far and wide,
For the prey he seeks,
There's no place to hide.

On wings as silent
As a summer breeze,
He disappears among
The trees.

Lewis Soanes (12)

The Seasons

In spring bulbs pop their heads up through the soil,
The beautiful colours of purple and yellow are soft like voile.
Summer brings an abundance of assorted shades of green,
With the sunshine glowing gold, it's fit for a queen.
Autumn comes, falling gracefully from the trees,
The ground is carpeted with copper, is covered with crisp leaves.
As winter arrives it brings a grey covering of frost,
Snowflakes fall, footprints and snowmen, it thaws and all is lost.
Our four seasons are so beautiful,
They come, go and change every day,
These are the colours of them all,
I love each of the seasons in different ways.

Alison Gilham (13)

The Sea

As the sun shines down onto the water, it sparkles like diamonds.
Softly and slowly it washes up onto the rocks.
Little whirlpools will slowly appear as the wind picks up,
As the wind becomes stronger, the whirlpool becomes bigger,
The waves become taller and stronger.
This can sometimes lead to storms,
The water crashes and smashes up against boats and sandbanks,
As the storm moves over, the sea calms down,
The whirlpools become smaller as the waves die down,
The sun comes out,
The warm water carries on washing upon the rocks.

Kailey Hunn (12)

Star

You wanna be a star?
Want to be rich with a nice car?
Want to be famous more than anything?
You want to act, model or sing?
Want to be a celebrity?

You're a superstar
Cameras follow you no matter where you are
Flash, flash in your face
All you want is some space
You are a celebrity

Tired, no more job offers
No more fighting through mobs of fans
No more money
You can't even afford a fake tan
You were a celebrity.

Kelsey Glover (12)

Birds Fly

Birds can fly super high,
When they fly in the rushing sky.

There's a sudden flee into the nearby tree,
Looking what there is to see.

Then *bang,* out it comes,
Soaring and boring lots of the people.

Birds, oh what wonderful things,
Their figure, colour and their wings.

Ben Carr (13)

Brian

Brian is a baddie,
As nasty as they come.
He terrifies his daddy
And mortifies his mum.

One morning in December,
They took him to the zoo,
But Brian lost his temper
And kicked a kangaroo.

Then he fought a lion,
Escaping from its pit,
It tried to swallow Brian,
Till Brian swallowed it!

Yes, Brian is a devil,
A horrid little curse -
Unlike his brother, Neville
Who's infinitely worse!

Bradley Hack (13)

Animal Motion

The cheetah runs swiftly after its prey,
catching food for its family each day.
The tortoise taking a long time
to get from one place to another.
Baby ducks swim close to their mother.
Snakes slithering across the ground.
Termites scurry to the top of their mound.
The eagle soaring through the sky,
spreading its wings, flying high.

Sarah Kelf (12)

I Wish

I wish I was a bird
Flying in the sky
I wish I was a bird
The world would pass by

I wish I was a fish
Swimming in the sea
I wish I was a fish
Feeling fresh and free

I wish I was a snail
Leaving trails of slime
I wish I was a snail
Not wasting any time

I wish I was the world
That's where I'd stay
I wish I was the world
But maybe another day.

Zoey Allen (12)

The Ocean

Down below in the ocean deep,
Where the creatures below hardly sleep,
The whales, the fish and the dolphins too,
Swim and glide like no one knew,
Peace and harmony will always reign,
Because no one knows their little game
Of hide-and-seek in the ocean blue,
They have an Eden they hide from you,
So don't try to find them,
Oh no you don't,
There's only one way,
That will have to wait until another day!

Jennifer Lee (13)

Guardian Angel

Young girl, don't cry, you know I'll be here
As your world starts to fall,
I'll be here to take your pain,
I'll help you try to forget it all.

I know you've been hurt,
I can see your pain,
But you're safe with me,
You'll never be abandoned or unloved again.

Young girl, it's all over now,
You're in a much happier place,
The beasts have gone, you can now be strong,
With no marks left across your face.

What happened hurt, but it happened for the best,
For you life will now be a whirl,
As where you are now is happy and safe
And you can rest in peace with me now, young girl.

Jade Russell (14)

Eagle

An eagle soars around the sky,
Searching for its prey,
Wing outstretched,
He weaves in and out looking about all day,
He spots his prey along the ground,
Wings pounding he swoops down,
His talons open as he grabs his prey,
His head moving side to side as he takes the mouse apart.

Samantha Laurie (12)

Football

Getting changed, shirts, shorts and socks,
Bell rings, players out on the pitch,
Captains in the middle, coin toss,
Whistle goes, kick-off.
Home team on the attack, pressure on the defence,
Attacker shoots - it's a goal! 1-0 up.
Whistle goes, half-time already,
Manager calls them for a team talk,
Time up, second-half kicks off,
Home team on the attack.
Foul! It's a penalty,
Striker steps up, shoots,
It's a goal, 2-0.
Referee looks at his watch,
Whistle in his hand, puts it in his mouth,
He blows, full-time,
Fans going wild.

Joe Wallis (13)

My Poem

Emotions, emotions, emotions,
Just feels like the ocean,
Some days the ocean goes up and down,
I just love the sound,
People are a lot like the ocean,
Some days they can be good then bad,
Happy or sad,
The little white bits on top of the waves,
Saves the day,
I would pay anything to watch the ocean,
Emotions, emotions, emotions.

Melissa Parr (12)

Sadness

Sadness is like your still beating heart being ripped out,
It feels as if no one cares,
It makes you feel like you are invisible,
Sadness is always getting you down,
It makes you feel like you're screaming as loud as you can
But you know no one is listening,
It feels like there is nothing left,
No hope, no joy and no purpose in life,
It's like a rainy day with the thick black storm clouds
Blocking out the sunlight and choking the life from your body,
Sometimes it makes you want to break down and cry
And let your life pass by without a blink of an eye,
Let it pass through your fingers,
You turn your back on life and walk away
Without even looking back or saying a word,
Sadness is the beginning of the end.

Rebecca Clay (13)

Autumn

Trees, trees, leaves on trees
They fall through autumn, come back summer
Leaves are green
And are crunchy
I love playing with them through the autumn

Jumping and rolling through the grass
Spiky and tall
It doesn't matter even if you fall
And overall autumn *rules!*

Sian Keeler (12)

Beautiful

We are human beings with feelings,
If someone hurts us, don't we cry?
But if not on the outside, we are all beautiful inside.
People get bullied if they're different,
Skin colour, religion or even different hair,
Just because of the difference, people will laugh, point and stare,
There is no need for it,
If someone calls us something - don't we hurt?
People get treated like they're nothing, like they're pieces of dirt.
People with braces, people with different faces,
People who are really tall,
People who are fat, people who are thin,
Even people who are very small,
But just remember one thing, if not on the outside,
We are all beautiful inside.

Iesha O'Brien (14)

The Runner

A runner is a swift moving person,
His motion is so smooth,
He shows great determination,
A lot he has to prove.
Oh my gosh, he is so fast,
There is simply no person that has been that fast,
There they go in the race,
But surely he will win first place.
When he wins the race,
He then knows that he goes along at a steady pace,
His name is Lloyd Howard
And he is motion powered.

Lloyd Howard (12)

The Sea

I stand on the beach
And look at the sea,
It's grey and dirty
And too cold for me.

The waves are high,
Splashing around,
I run and jump in,
Until I can feel my feet touch the ground.

The sound of the sea
Can be soothing and calm,
But when it turns rough,
You could be alarmed.

The waves will roll
And sounds echo around,
I need to get out,
Feel my feet touch the ground.

I sit on the sand
And quietly listen,
The sound of the ocean
And seeing it glisten.

Siobhan Harkins (12)

I Miss You

Even though we are far apart
You are always here in my heart
I think about you every day
And all the things I'd like to say
Though a mile between us lie
I'd like to send a hug and a hi.

Claire Keyzor (14)

Poetry In Motion

Waiting on the grid,
Engines groaning,
All waiting for the lights to go out!

The tensions mounting,
Hearts are pounding
And the crowds are shouting out.

Lights go out,
Without a doubt,
Whilst the roaring of the engines echo all about.

The cars speed on,
Like bullets from a gun,
Only now the race has begun!

They are battling for position,
In this competition,
Who has the determination to win?

You can smell the fuel and burning rubber,
As they all race against each other.

Coming to the end,
Around the next bend,
Who will taste the victory
And go down in history?

Only the chosen few
Will go through!

Jemma Minshull (12)

Love

As I see you
With the sun in your hair,
I can't help but
Stop and stare.

As I see you
With a twinkle in your eye,
It reminds me of
Stars in the sky.

As I see you
With a smile on your face,
I can see your
Inner grace.

As I see you
Walking past, I'm so shy
I run away
Fast.

Jon Taylor (12)

A Poem About Motion

Motion
I stride
I am wandering
Through the woods
I glide along the ice
Roll in the snow
I have movement
I stride
Motion.

Malcolm Brown (12)

Death

Death is so far, but so close,
We don't know when our time has come,
Young, old or middle-aged,
Either of them, people dread it.
People want it to come faster,
But none of them know what it's like
Beyond Earth!

Rebeka Austin (12)

Twilight

The night was young,
The clouds were hanging around,
Waiting for the night sky.
The cold spring rain is falling,
Out in the lonely tree
A slight wind rustled the leaves,
The street lights flickered,
Scaring the midnight animals,
Which have just woken,
From their winter's hibernation.

Lewis Nicholas (13)

Whirly Wind

When I go walking in the fields,
I fly my kite in the wind,
Ducking, diving, left and right,
I give the people such a fright,
But when it's still I have to say,
The kite is trash so throw it away!

William Beevor (12)

Four Walls And A Door

The walls are bare
Damp and dark
I feel so cold
Why aren't you here?

I'm paying my time in an awful place
Don't throw away the key
I want to be released

Let me out, I cry all day
I am so lonely
So trapped behind bars
This is a torturing punishment

Now I've done my time
I am free
Smell the freshness
All over again.

Chloe Hood (13)

Tigers

Tigers hide in the long lime-green grass
Waiting for a yummy deer to pass,
Tigers, tigers, tigers.

Tigers are beautiful and their fur is smooth,
As the wind blows each will move,
Tigers, tigers, tigers.

Tigers sprawl themselves in the shade away from the sun,
Watching their cubs playing and having fun,
Tigers, tigers, tigers.

Kirsten Abel (12)

Cats

Cats purr and prance with pride,
As if they were the king of the castle.
As they walk they sway jauntily,
Swaying from side to side letting their fur stand up on end.

Laying peacefully, they wrap their tail around your leg,
Laying and waiting for your hand to stroke them.
Stroking, stroking, how they love the attention,
Poking, poking, how they hate it.

They sit so elegant, sitting, waiting to pounce,
Waiting, watching, focusing on a mouse across the room.
Suddenly, before you know it, the cat pounces, chases,
The mouse is caught, dinner!
Sleepy, sleepy, time to rest.

Liane Mansfield (12)

Surf's Up!

The summer's here so surf is up,
I've waited all winter to win this cup.
The comp comes soon and I'm rigid with fear,
But the sea is more water than Mum's little tear.

I go on out into the ocean,
All I need is courage potion,
But it all goes well, I'm still alive,
On the shore Brad gives me five.

The judges score me ten, ten, ten,
I'd done better than the men.
So I go on home, put my cup on the shelf,
I felt so proud, I'd done this all by myself!

Kerry Moore (13)

The Rogue Slayer!

She is the one who is built to kill,
Born with bravery, power and skill
And who dares to challenge her surely will die,
Then six feet under they will lie.
If looks could kill she would be the best,
Terrorising the good like a vicious blood-fest.
Though she acts nice then turns to a player,
She is the one, she is the roger slayer.

Lewis Smith (13)

Waves

At sunset the waves crash
Against the rough rocks
Like white horses full of rage

The salty water glistens
As the steam shoots up

As the waves slow down
Trickling salt comes back down from the rocks
And meets back with the water.

Danielle Supocko (12)

Swimming

S pectating parents watching anxiously as the whistle blows.
W himpering children that haven't done so well.
I mpatient people waiting for results.
M otionless children waiting to swim.
M eaningful cheers from friends and family.
I mportant times waiting to be received.
N aughty sneers at opponents' times.
G loating comments to your rivals.

Oliver Lee (13)

Freedom Of The Sea

They glide through the calm seas,
As the sun glistens upon the water,
They fly across the soft and gentle skies.

Their playful games and smiley faces,
Amaze sightseers in every way.

How I'd like to be one of these,
A dolphin's life is just for me.

Sophie Burgess (12)

Water Motion

Water comes and water goes,
Water drips and water flows,
Water's here and water's there,
It's absolutely everywhere,
It trickles down on rocky ground
And makes a splashing sound,
Water tumbles over rocks,
Cascading to the ground.

Elizabeth Paine (12)

Manic Machine

Arms moving up, down, side to side,
Steam billowing,
Pistons moving in and out,
Wheels spinning.

Wooden beams up and down,
Leather strap side to side,
Flow of cotton feeding in,
Linen flowing out.

Christopher Ball (12)

Friends

Friends are for being there and caring too,
Friends are there to have fun with you!
They share their secrets and never tell . . .
The stories of fun and laughter as well!

Sophie and Synayde are two of my friends,
With them I have fun that never ends,
Without my friends I don't know what I'd do . . .
No friends in the world, not even a few!

We all had a fight but it didn't last,
We solved our differences very fast . . .
We've joined our hearts and stuck together;
Now our friendship will be remembered forever!

Amanda Elliott (13)

The Runaway

I had thought about it all night
And it gave me an awful fright,
I crept around at eleven o'clock,
I got all ready but forgot my sock,
I got outside in a flash,
Then I heard an awful crash,
It was my brother sleepwalking,
I could even hear him talking,
They ran outside because they knew I was missing,
These people across the road were even kissing,
On the moped I had got,
Then I went off in a shot.

Harley Clements (12)

The Jungle

In the jungle I try to find,
An animal, who is gentle and kind . . .

I feed the tiger, put ants in a tub,
Oh, how I long to find a nice gentle cub.

In the jungle I'm looking for,
An animal as big as his roar . . .

I crawl under the elephant, run away from a bear,
Look! A lion is growling right over there.

I tried to care for the animals,
I tried to be brave . . .
But at this very moment, it's me I have to save!

Kelsey Janisch (12)

Living It Up!

We can stare and we can glare
We will do anything we dare
We can jump and we can thump
We can also make a bump
We can splash and we can thrash
Because we can run as quick as a flash
We can walk and we can talk
We can yap and we can rap
We can move and we can groove
We can dance and we can prance
We whisper secrets we can keep
But best of all, we can sleep!

Jessica Turrell (12)

The Flying Feline

As still as a statue
The watching cat,
Jerks her head sharply;
To see a vibrating butterfly.

Slowly she crawls,
Ready to pounce
And soars through the air;
Like a springing spider monkey.

Up raised its paw
And the butterfly flew,
Quivering its wings in excitement;
Leaving the leaping cat solitary.

Kimberley Fowler (13)

His Motion

He jumped and he spun,
He moved all around,
He ran and he sprang,
He smiled and frowned.
He swam,
He dived,
He likes to jive,
He sprints,
He sings,
He does his things,
His motions.

Daniel Savage (13)

Moving House

I took one last look
Around my old home,
Everything was packed,
Even the garden gnome.

To see it all bare,
Made me feel quite sad,
All the happy memories,
Of the fun times we'd had.

We needed more room,
So Mum and Dad said,
A big bedroom for me,
With a four-poster bed.

I've seen the new house,
Mum took me there twice
And I had to agree,
That it was very nice.

The house I was leaving
Would stay in my heart,
But it really was exciting
To make a new start.

We've been here a year now
And it's easy to see,
How happy I am
Living here with my family!

Erin Nightingale (12)

Run Rabbit Run!

My bunny jumps high and low
Where she goes, nobody knows
Skipping on the grass
Rushing through and through
Suddenly she stops to have a little rest
And spots a bird up in its nest
The bird glides off into the deep blue sky
My bunny thinks she can get it but it's just too high
Faster and faster the bird flies away
Never mind bunny thought, *I'll race with it another day.*

Jasmine Esherwood (12)

Mermaid Of The Sea

As I swim through the sea
I hear its call
As I splash and float
But as much as I like it
I cannot leave
I am a mermaid, cold of heart
And I love the sea
As it breaks and crashes against the rocks
And pours to the softly flowing streams.

Sara Bone (12)

The Sea

An early morning wake up as waves bind together,
With ripples as white as snow,
Midday approaching as waves begin to erode the cliffs like sharks,
As the evening draws in, it starts to twinkle like millions of stars,
As evening ends it is so quiet as it finally gets some rest.

Mitch Forbes (13)

The Beast

The great machine's engines breathing like a beast,
It rumbled through the deserted city, waiting for its prey.

Suddenly three bikes rushing towards the tank blazing bolters
Ricocheting off the armour.
The guns of the tank burst into life,
Blowing apart two bikes and sending the third bike skidding into
The beast's tracks and only moved the beast an inch.
The tank then crashed through the crushed bones of the enemy.
The great beast came to a halt
And turned the head-like turret to a great building,
The beast roared up its cannons
And the blinding shot streaked across the battle-scarred road
And it slammed into the building bringing the building
Down in a massive dust cloud.
The beast turned and carried on its way.

Jake Boggis (13)

Avalanche

It doesn't matter if it's a shout or a pin drop
It dislodges snow and starts an avalanche off
The twisting and twirling snow
Starts heading down, nowhere it can't go
It sweeps away anything in its path
You can't run - it's going too fast!
It's too late, it's taken you away
Your eyelids close, shutting out the day
You can't feel anything but the cold
You don't survive - your story never to be told.

Andrew Petersen (14)

Waves

Waves,
A god of all the seas,
A cantankerous army controlled by weather,
Its roaring voice creates a mighty din,
Acrobatic feats crash against the rocks.

A surfer's dream,
A fisherman's living,
A lifeguard's nightmare,
All human beings place their fate
In the rough and dangerous territory of a wave.

In summer waves are calm,
In autumn waves begin to stir,
In winter waves become turbulent and vigorous
And in the spring they turn solitary and quiet.

Ben Grey (13)

The Car In Motion

The car is so fast,
You never know where it goes,
Sometimes it crashes,
Sometimes it rolls.

Pink, blue, yellow or green,
With those bright colours,
It will always be seen.

The car is so fast,
You never know where it goes,
Sometimes it crashes,
Sometimes it rolls.

Sophie Parrott (12)

The Boy Racer

The door slammed shut
Foot pressed down with all his might
The engine revved and roared
With tyres burning, it was an awesome sight

Music blared and thundered
Smoke from the wheels choked the air
The sound of sixteen hundred horses
Was like a dragon leaving its lair

Behind silver shades his eyes glinted and gleamed
Down the straight without a backward glance
Concentration etched on every bit of his face
One false move and the car would surely dance

No time for anything
Not even a smile
A lapse in judgement
Would cost him a mile

The needle reached a hundred
His goal was met
Now a smile on his face
His target was set!

Blue lights flashing
Sirens pounding in his head
The game was over
Now he was dead!

Silence and stillness filled the air
The engine now softly purring
Smoke billowing swiftly
Wheels once racing now only whirring.

Edward Warner (12)

Advance

Advance!
Tanks ground into action,
Troops' boots started to move through the deep mud,
Another order was shouted up into the dewy morning air,
Men ran,
Tanks sped up,
Gunshots fired,
Their guns had to be silenced
And so it began.

Tom Gaskin (12)

Turning 18

Now that I've turned 18, I look back and see,
That my childhood was brief,
It was all over much too quickly,
I miss being young and carefree,
Too many people have already come and gone in my life,
But this is an ongoing journey,
We can remember the past fondly,
But we cannot cling onto it forever,
I look ahead to my new life,
Eighteen, driving, going to university,
There seems endless possibilities,
Who knows where my choices will take me in the next eighteen years,
My childhood has become a closed chapter,
Yet I hope that I always remain full of love and hope,
As I was when I was a young girl,
Growing up isn't easy, but I'm learning.

Carys Jones (18)

The Sad Reality Of Life

As your body and soul rest after a hectic day,
Your mind asleep beings to awaken, wander and play,
It leaves its daily dense confines
And enters a world of abstract findings.
You find yourself in the midst of fantastic creatures,
Or in a palm's shade on one of Phuket's many beaches.
Your body off on a distant mountain,
Your mind forgetting the clock's counting.
It is truly a gift from God to be given such sleep,
One that is so tranquil, so vivid, so deep,
Sleep is a beauty that cannot be seen, only felt
And lost so quickly when Mom abruptly throws off the covers
And the spears of the cold attack you,
You then face a whole day back in the sad reality of life.

Jonathan Forsgren (16)

Life

I look around . . . nothing
dark, isolation, fright.
I am alone . . .
alone in my thoughts . . .
alone in my world.
Nobody.
This thing that everybody calls *life*
has been going on for too long.
This has to end
once and for all . . .

Othmane Bargach (16)

The Fight

Butterflies floating in my stomach,
As I enter the ring,
Staring in his eyes,
When the bell goes 'ding',
Rendering right look to the ribs,
Then the crowd sing.

Round two starts,
Thinking I'd won round one,
Struck a hook to the head,
Like Mike Tyson,
I'm already tired,
And he looks dizzy,
So I finish him off,
And his eyes go fizzy,
He fell to the canvas,
And the ref starts counting,
But you couldn't really hear him,
By the crowds loud shouting.

He counted to ten,
That made me happy,
But not for the baby (opponent),
He was crying in his nappy,
The crowd was cheering,
For me Scotty-C,
The champion of the world,
Is no more Ali!

Scotty Cordle (14)

Passing Storm

Gentle rustling, leaves are moving
Branches dipping in the breeze
Signs of stronger weather stirring
Up amongst the trees

Heavy rain clouds, sun extinguished
Changes now to jet-black sky
Rumbling thunder in the distance
Flashing lightning racing by

Bending, cracking, breaking branches
Tearing leaves from where they grow
Howling, screeching, unrelenting
Will this storm ever go?

Finally it is gently easing
Slowing down, it begins to cease
Quieter, calmer – trees stop moving
Storm has passed – returned to peace.

Sarah Roberts (13)

Going Through Life

When I was born, I was happy and carefree
I went whenever, wherever for a wee

As I got older the trouble came
I said it wasn't me I still got the blame

When I was a young adult, I went over the top
I drank one too many alcopop

Ten years later I became more responsible
I had to keep paying bill after bill

That's my life story through and told
Because now I'm old, crippled and bald.

Nicholas Gillett (13)

The Great North Run

The Great North Run
Is so much fun
Smiling faces
Take their places
Waiting for the starter's gun

Off they go
Some are slow
Others are fast
One will be last
But they're all enjoying it so

The weather is fine
Along the Tyne
They're dressed up as clowns
Raising pounds and pounds
But where is the finishing line?

Now it's the end
Round the final bend
Crowds are cheering
The post is nearing
Cash to charity they'll send.

Stephen Muncaster (13)

The Roller Coaster

As I sit here, my head spinning around,
I then look at the ground
And the world is upside down.

As I sit here the wind blowing against my hair,
Like the trees in the cold March air,
Then people stop and stare.

As I sit here alone, in a crowd,
The noise is so deafeningly loud,
From the riders so proud.

Laura Hayes (12)

The Sports Car

A car in motion,
A man's devotion,
With much pollution
And no solution.

I travel far,
In my sports car,
A different colour,
Like no other.

My passenger's smelly,
Who's sick as jelly!
Passing plants and trees
And bumblebees.

The end became nigh,
With a tear in my eye,
As I returned home,
For the end of my poem.

James Cuffe (13)

Dream Holiday

I'm going on a holiday
I'm going on a trip
To a place where it's sunny
And it's very still
Where the ocean is blue
And all the trees are green
It's a tropical place
I'm excited to go there
You can watch birds fly high
Or fish that never die
You can do what you want
Go swimming or just walk
It's a magical place
Wouldn't you like to come?

Maria Guisasola (13)

Fairground Attractions

I got out of the car
And walked down the street
Wondering if there would be
Any cartoon characters to meet

I entered the fair
And looked at the rides
Lots of people were queuing there
Side by side

With clothes of blue, red, orange and green
Shining so bright
They were sure to be seen
Even in the starlight

I was in the arcade
With fruit machines flashing
People winning money
And teenagers bashing

I went on the Ferris wheel
The roller coaster too
Then my dad said, 'Let's go for a burger,'
And I said, 'True, true, true.'

Tom Bird (13)

Slalom Haiku

Speeding down the slope,
In a cloud of icy spray,
Slicing through the cold.

Alex Ormerod (12)

Showtime!

The eerie impostor I saw in my reflection,
The grease paint wouldn't help my complexion.
I wriggled on my bloomers and yanked on my hat,
I didn't like that costume, I looked like a prat.

What would all the school kids say
When they watched the show today?
I can't back out, it's too late now,
I would make myself look better, if I knew how!

This was it, I would be on show,
After the five minutes we had to go.
The atmosphere was full of fear,
As the overture we all did hear.

The stage director called me up,
As I stared at the water in my cup.
I wolfed it down and held my heart,
As the National Anthem made its start.

The curtain opened, I was revealed,
But my fate in this show was sadly sealed,
So I struck my pose and held my breath,
After all it's hard to act out death!

Philippa Shellard (13)

Wind Haiku

Leaves are getting blown,
Trees swaying violently in
The howling, strong wind.

David Hodgson (12)

The Race

The crowd was cheering
I was ready to go,
All that stopped me
Was the horn's first blow.

All stood so still,
My heart pounding fast,
Leaning so forward,
No one's getting past.

Beep and they're off,
Let's keep it steady,
Don't lose your breath,
Fast when ready.

Nearly there now,
Not long to go,
I see the line,
Oh no! My toe.

I fall to the ground
And cry a big yelp,
No one comes,
So I cry for help.

They pull me up
And I look around,
No one's there,
No tapping sound.

I start to run,
The pain in my spine,
I hear the gun
And I've crossed the line!

It doesn't seem real,
I've won the race,
I can't believe
I've gained first place.

Rosie Cottam (13)

Getting Away From It All

They were always fighting,
I had to get away from it,
I needed to escape.

I ran to my room
And put on some clothes
And all the money I owned into a bag.

I left a note telling them I would be fine,
I walked out of the door
And took one last look at my home.

I was on my way, on my own,
Never going back,
I told myself I could survive.

I had walked for hours in the cold,
I started feeling tired,
I sat in a shelter and cried.

I woke up the next morning,
I had survived a night on my own,
I was fine; I had to keep on going.

I walked for the whole day
And spent the night thinking,
I knew I was never going back.

They might be worried about me,
But really, I'm fine,
I am feeling a bit lonely though.

I will keep on running
And I'll get used to the cold,
I have managed so far.

They were always fighting,
I got away from it all,
I had finally escaped.

Sarah Boardman (13)

The Most Important Journey Of My Life!

I remember seeing it,
Hearing it even,
It was coming for me,
Like a bird after prey!

I felt it hit me,
The pain was unbearable,
But then nothing,
It was all over,
I couldn't feel a thing!

My body went limp,
I could work out a shape
In front of me,
It was bright,
Blinding to look at!

At that point something clicked,
I suddenly knew what was happening,
I had been run over
And I was making that famous journey,
The one everyone wonders about,
The one to a better place!

Joanne Scott (13)

The Crash

I lie there dreaming when suddenly I hear screaming,
My sister is scared by a loud smash,
I look outside to the scene of a crash.
My car is in the middle without a scrape,
But my neighbour's car is smashed into my gate.
The other car's roof is caved in but there are no people within.
My mum rings the police, it takes them 7 minutes,
I shout out of the window, 'Good job there's nobody in it!'
Looking at my watch, it's 5am,
I know I'll never get back to sleep again . . .

Thomas Powell (12)

Criminal

Coming out the murder scene
In his flash new car
Soon on the motorway
Ripping up tar

With the police on his trail
And a body in the trunk
No one could catch up
To the criminal punk

Moving quickly on the chase
Over speeds of 90 miles per hour
Police closing in, pedal to the metal
Speeding through a hailstorm shower

Crashing into a roundabout
Soon into a hospital bed
But not so long after
That criminal lay dead!

Lee Burns (13)

River Poem

I'm running fast down the hill,
Over the rocks I'm running still
The faster I flowed
The more I erode
I start to swerve from side to side
As the river slows I start to glide
Transporting rocks, pebbles, sand and silt
Depositing them on a tilt
My journey has come to an end
As I turn the final bend
As I meet up with the sea
Eternal friends we will always be.

Nathaniel McCormack (12)

The Pendulum

The proud pendulum swings,
As changes come and go.
Everything around it,
Is just part of the show.

But still the pendulum swings.

Another child is born,
One more beat of the heart.
Human race develops,
Each person plays their part.

But still the pendulum swings.

Civilisations rise,
Civilisations fall,
But the pendulum glides,
Without a care at all

And yet the pendulum swings.

David Sleeman (13)

The Football Match

Gathered crowds around the ground,
Lots of songs and sounds.
Through the turnstile we go,
As we watch the people flow.
We take our seats for this football treat,
As the players are announced you can feel the heat.
The whistle blows the match begins.

I can't believe I am here, watching these men the best in their careers.
The skill is brill, they have no fears.
One pass to another and then there were cheers.
Yes, there is a goal!
The full time whistle blows, we jump for joy,
We clap our hands; we have just watched the best team in the land.

Christopher Ray (12)

Poetry In Motion

On the first day that I was born
The first thing that I saw was you
There wasn't much that I could do
But still you smiled and cried with glee

Sometime later I was three
All I did was play with toys
Like cars and bricks and plastic toys
And soon I would discover more new tricks

A few years later I was six
And learned to ride my bike
Now I didn't have to hike
And I was filled with joy through and through

Now I've been given lots of things by you
But not everyone's lucky like me
I was always filled with glee
So thanks for being a special mum
And making me a talented son.

Adam Hobson (13)

Hallowe'en

The army marches up the path,
Big carrier bags full of sweets,
They ring the bell with anticipation,
Hoping for some treats.

The sky as dark as velvet,
Ghosts and ghouls everywhere.
Children scattered like a jigsaw puzzle,
Trying to spook and scare.

The witches, skeletons and vampires,
Are the scariest things you've ever seen.
When the fireworks no longer boom,
It's the end of Hallowe'en.

Lauren Jones (12)

The Banger

Going slow,
Going fast,
See those cars just flying
Past;

Some red,
Some green,
Some so fast they can't be
Seen;

Some sporty,
Some flash,
Some going with a
Dash;

Nearly there,
Almost done,
It's been good this ride such
Fun.

But, now we're there,
We've reached the end,
As we turn this final
Bend;

The car I'm in
It really is bad,
It embarrasses me but not my
Dad;

He thinks it's great,
That it's really top brand,
My mum doesn't though, it cost her
Four grand.

Michael Wallace (13)

Sea Dance

The rush of her feet
And the swish of her skirt
The sway makes the audience
Become aware and alert

They swivel and turn
Until they are safe
From the splash of her shoes
From the dancing rage

The splash of the music
As she swifts across the floor
The sand swirls around her
They watch in awe

As she swivels and turns
And the sand grains prance
The audience cheer
The amazing sea dance.

Elissa Thackwray (12)

The Swan

Almost still in the sky,
Gracefully gliding by,
Its wings stretched out proud,
Flying as high as a cloud.

So clumsily on the ground,
Green grass all around,
Her feathers silky and white,
Eyes dark, dark as the night.

She slips into the water without any sound,
She looks to see if her friends are around,
There they are, on the other side of the lake,
I wonder how long to catch them she will take.

Kate Cottam (12)

I Want To Be A Grown-Up, I Don't Want To Be A Kid!

Life is such a journey
It goes on for ages
People are not always the same
We grow up in stages

I suppose when we're born
We don't have a journey at all
Babies don't do much like you and me
They cry all the time and they can see

But they don't do a lot you know it's true
They're not educated like me or you
I don't know why but I really do care
I want to be older, it's just not fair!

I want to be a grown-up, I don't want to be a kid anymore!

I could go to the future and be older, I've got a time machine, let's go!
It worked, I'm in the future, oh my goodness,
Many kids! I work day and night! No time for myself!
I've just been to the future, that's what my life will be about.

Now the future I have been,
I don't want to be a grown-up,
I want to stay thirteen!

Rachel Gee (13)

Football Frenzy

The sun was shining, a beautiful day,
To go out on the football pitch and play.
The teams march out, each player overweight,
If they sat on a roof, they'd break the slate!
The pitch is boggy, churned up, a disgrace,
A big blob of fat falls flat on his face.
The man screams, 'Foul!' No foul given,
He hunts his prey, determined, driven.
A swing of his leg, hacks down his prey,
He's shown the red card, that's the end of his day.
There's a big red gash on the victim's ankle,
'If that's all he's got, he should be thankful!'
The man walks away, his face very grave,
Then smiles, 'That's what you get when you mess with Dave!'
The sky turns grey, it's misty and dim,
As puffy black rain clouds shadow over him,
So victim, when you're lying down there in pain,
The man who hacked you's getting soaked in the rain!

Michael Hall (12)

Falling

I am falling through the air,
But I don't know what to do,
I have only 30 seconds,
Until I experience something new.

I feel my life is going to change,
I do not want to die,
I want to be really very rich
And buy what I can buy.

With thousands of people watching me,
High in the air like a jumping bean,
As I bounce as high as I possibly can,
On my winning trampoline.

Emma Cinis (12)

Wind

The wind blew hard and fast,
It knocked over a man in a body cast.
The wind picked up as I walked down the street,
I felt a chill at the bottom of my feet.

The wind was like a slap in the face,
I soon began to pick up the pace.
I saw a tree snap straight in half,
It almost landed on a baby calf.

I opened my door
And fell straight to the floor.
I thought, *what a day this has been*
And what horrible things I have seen.

Finally the day had ended,
The wind had stopped and trees were mended.

Steven Bassett (12)

The Bully!

He hit me hard on the cheek,
This big lad was certainly not weak.
He said, 'After school so everyone can see.'
I didn't know why he had chosen me.
When the bell rang after school,
I thought this lad is really cruel.
I saw him standing at the gates,
With all his very big, hard mates.
I couldn't handle this anymore,
So I ran home and headed straight for the door.
I tripped and fell and grazed my knee,
So he ran over and helped me.
I didn't understand why he had done this,
But at least now I wouldn't have to tell Miss.
He said he'd check up on me and give me a call,
Maybe this lad wasn't so bad after all.

Angela Cartmell (13)

The Running Man

Motion is fast,
Motion is slow,
You could be an amateur
Or even a pro.

Jogging through the street,
Jogging through the town,
Doing it to the beat,
In your mother's dressing gown.

Looking very dumb,
Acting like a clown,
Sucking your thumb,
Whilst you run up and down.

The end is near,
The red tape is in sight,
It is so clear,
My future is bright.

Daniel Coughlin (13)

Autumn

Autumn leaves sway to the ground,
As the bloodthirsty wind circles by,
With a fighting storm ahead of him,
Making sure summer has died.

Autumn's quickly brewing,
Say the animals who shake,
Quivering plants with their newborn buds
Are too afraid to stretch and wake.

It looks like snow will be falling fast,
Which will make snowball fighting start,
In autumn my fire is my best friend,
We'll never be apart.

Nicola Gee (12)

Pictures In Motion

I work with pictures in motion
And my job is full of commotion
I work in a messy cinema
And the pay won't buy a wheel of a car
The punters leave the place in a mess
So I can't do the cleaning in my Sunday best
There's always cans and popcorn all over the floor
And the greedy brats always go back for more
I'm sick of doing this pathetic job
I can't even afford some corn on the cob
I'm giving up and I don't know what to do
I can't stand the smell of the stinky loo
I've finally taken to desperate measures
Time to bring out one of my little treasures
It's now hidden under a middle row seat
It'll be one big job for the bobby on the beat
I hope it doesn't get found before it goes off
Or my hands will be locked in metal handcuffs
I should get mounds of compensation
The tragedy should be on every TV station
It should go off when it's not my shift
I wonder how far the smoke will drift?
I'm now sat at home drinking a cup of Bovril
And the cat is asleep on the window sill
It should go off very, very soon
Right in the middle of The Aliens of Doom
I flick on the TV and guess what I see?
It's only Coronation Street
I put Ceefax on but there's nothing there
I think I'll just resign; I don't really care
I suddenly hear a tick, tick, tick
I must be imagining it; I'm getting on a bit
It's coming from under the kitchen sink
I think I need to have a drink
Tick, tick, tick, tick, tick, tick
Tick, tick, tick, tick, tick, tick

I open the cupboard and nearly die of shock
It's not under a middle row seat
The bomb's underneath my kitchen sink
Tick, tick, tick, tick, tick, tick
Tick, tick, tick, tick, tick, tick
Oh no! *Bang!*
One week later I looked at my 'home'
There is nothing left, not even a phone
There's only rubble left of my house
And the body of my little dead pet mouse
It's all my fault though
Now I've nowhere to go
If I wasn't so evil with a bad memory
Then I'd still have a lock to insert my key.

Sinéad Heneghan (13)

The Train

The familiar noise of the train approaches,
The big, black, bulky monster pulls into the station.
The eager passengers pick up luggage and suitcases,
'All aboard.'
The platform clears as a sea of people spill into
The small doors of the train,
The train departs leaving an eerie silence in its wake,
Slowly it picks up speed,
It moans and groans as it climbs up a steep hill,
Slowly, slowly and then it zooms down,
On a seemingly never-ending journey it carries on into the distance,
The eternal voyager with no destination,
It moved along the horizon like a slithering snake,
Inside all is quiet as people sit,
Glued to the beautiful scenery rushing past them,
Through small villages and towns it ran not stopping for anything,
Then it slows, slows, slows to a snail's pace
And all is quiet as the passengers silently depart
As the journey begins once again.

Malachy Shellard (15)

I Hate Trains

I hate trains,
The nattering noise of the engine,
(Is my brother and sisters shouting and screaming),
Oh my head.

I hate trains,
The outside makes me feel sick,
Everything is blurred and moving fast.

I hate trains,
Bump! Bump!
Oh how I ache,
The tracks are rotten and old.

I hate trains,
Zoom! They go with all their might, hearts racing,
Arms and legs pushing to get to the finish line.

I hate trains,
I've arrived at last,
I'm never going on one of those
Terrible trains again.

Aimée Roberts (12)

Fire

Fire can be anywhere,
The orange, red and yellow flare.

Fire can blaze and fire can spin,
It keeps us warm in the world we're in.

Its flaming eyes are always flicking
And its fierce tail is quickly flicking.

Fire can be anywhere,
Destroying things without a care.

Fire can create a scare,
A serial killer, cold and bare.

Michael McKenna (12)

That Animal At The Zoo

The animal I like the best
With its trunk like a tree
And its ears like giant bed sheets,
Staring at me.

His feet are giant mushrooms,
Toenails big and white,
I tried to talk, transfixed and staring
At this beautiful, elegant sight.

People call them nature's masterpiece,
With their trunk swinging to and fro,
Beautiful animals with their tusks so big,
I wanted to stay here and never go.

With a swish of his tail,
He walks on by,
He walks with a thump
And nearly touches the sky.

This animal you have guessed
Is like a big balloon,
This animal is an elephant!
I'm coming back to see it soon!

Jennifer Fletcher (12)

My Father

He will always be with me wherever I go,
I will never forget him
And I will always love him.
When I am with my family, we laugh and cry about him,
We remember the good times and the bad times
And the times we laughed with him,
The pain is still there
And it will never leave,
I will never forget him,
He is my father.

Laura Cox (12)

I Could Play All Day!

I love to play
Out in the fresh air
Wind rushing through my hair
I could play all day

I love to play
With all my friends
Singing songs that never end
I could play all day

I love to play
Running round the yard
Falling over and being scarred
I could play all day

I love to play
On the playground
My friends make a great sound
I could play all day.

Melanie Fisher (12)

A Flea

I wish I could fly like a pie in the sky
And see all the sea with the eye of a bee
And wouldn't it be funny to eat all the honey
And have some left for tea
But most of all I would wish
To swim in the sea like a fish
Or jump up and down like a flea
To run like a dog and buzz like a bee
Wouldn't it be nice to be home for tea?
And then off again with my eye of a bee
And I wouldn't be lonely because
I've got my pet flea.

Isaac Ormond (12)

Snow

Silently, softly it falls,
Covering our house like a curtain,
No one escapes the winter
And snow makes that certain.

Silently, softly it falls,
Tiny little flakes of coldness.
Only children are playing outside,
Because they are filled with boldness.

Silently, softly it falls,
A fairy with magical dust,
Sprinkling it everywhere she goes,
Coming in one big gust.

Silently, softly it falls,
As white as a diamond ring,
It's cold and wet and it's good fun,
It's something the winter will bring.

Elizabeth Klenk (12)

The Identified Flying Object

There it was,
Hovering over land,
A silver slick object
Scanning the ground like an owl hunting its prey,
Silently spinning on its axes,
Scouring the Earth.
(Needing information for their leader.)
Gliding gracefully in the sky,
It comes to a halt.
Star-like lights flash randomly in the dark,
All at once, as if it's changed its mind,
It changes direction,
Piercing the atmosphere like an arrow,
Never to be seen again!

Joe Kelly (12)

I Am Ill

I was lying there,
Looking very hopeless,
Like a newborn baby,
Being very sleepless.

My head was a roller coaster,
Spinning because of that ill girl's fault,
Then suddenly it went *crash, bang, ping*
And it came to a halt.

I rushed downstairs in joy
And screamed across the street,
I'm not ill! I'm not ill!
And the wind swept me off my feet.

I flew and flew, in the autumn leaves
And soon I was as high as the birds,
I tried to touch the clouds and the beautiful sky,
But fell back down head-first.

Then with a fright I woke up
And realised it had all been a dream
And that I was still there lying,
As ill as a cut-off stream!

Mercedes De Pascual Cardiel (12)

Parachutes

As the light changes from red to green
My world stops
Cloud swirls around me
Galloping like dreams

Plane speeds away into the horizon
I'm falling at the speed of light
Colours are being washed away
Like an artist's paint palette

Land intertwines with sky
Clouds pull at their cords
White wispy ones curling
Grey bullies its way across

Waves of this swirling sea
Dance across me
Then the dream ends and
I'm falling

I've landed on my feet
Red and white lands beside
Their cords are withering snakes
It's amazing what you see at 15,000 feet!

Robin Campbell (12)

Autumn Goes By

Autumn is at last here,
Lonely birds sweetly trill,
Around all seems peaceful,
Many things aren't at rest.

The wind blows around us,
Like a silvery shawl,
It whispers through branches
And sweeps up their dead leaves.

The golden leaves falling,
Feathers tumbling down,
Gliding down swiftly as
Blossom swirls from a tree.

The birds cry as they fly,
Birds swooping and soaring,
Lightly spiralling down,
Then on their swift voyage.

A glorious sunset,
Lights the end of the day,
With warm amber colours,
Silently says goodnight.

Ana-Aquilina Hickford-Martinez (12)

Music

Music is around us everywhere
Just listen to the beat
Some people sitting over there
Are tapping with their feet

The beat, the beat
The beat of the music
Is very important you see
Cos if you ain't got the beat
Then you can't move your feet
Then no one will be on the dance floor

There are
Artists like Michael Jackson
Who have sold a lot of records
His songs have a lot of rhythm
And beat, there is even more

The beat, the beat
The beat of the music
Is very important you see
Cos if you ain't got the beat
And you can't move your feet
Then your song won't sell any records.

Jack Shields (12)

Light

Light is all around you
Light is in your head
Light is in your eyes
Light makes dark look dead

It shines in different colours
It shines high and low
It shines through the darkness
It shines and makes a glow

Without light there is darkness
Without light there is cold
Without light there is no life
Without light there's nothing to be told

Light shines around the world
Light shines over land and sea
Light gives us hope and faith
For all of us to see.

Philip Armitstead (12)

The Beach

The long stretch of golden sand,
The waves crashing against the rocks,
The sound of children screaming and shouting
Like the animals at the zoo.
The warm feeling of the sand rubbing against your feet
As you walk into the sea,
The gentle breeze blowing through the palm trees,
Like the sound of people whispering.
The clear blue sky with the golden sun beaming on us
And at the end of the day when the beach is empty
The orange sun sets upon the sea.

Ella Crumpton (12)

The Garden

In the garden it's like a rainbow
Seeing colour wherever I go

The roses are white and red
But I fear some might be dead

The poppies are the most beautiful I ever saw
They bring back memories of the war

As I walk past
I can see the daisies growing fast

The tulips light the garden with such power
As they are my favourite flower

I can see the sunflowers reaching up high
Almost touching the sky

When I leave the garden it begins to rain
I can see the plants growing from down the lane.

Leigh Owen (12)

On The Move

Celebs are always on the move,
not much time to groove,
too much work to be done,
has anyone got a gun?

Tours, awards and photo shoots,
never any time to shoot some hoops,
celebs are always on the move,
not much time to groove!

Movies, music, stage and lights,
bet they wouldn't mind a Sunny Delight!
Aussie, Florida, Russia too
and at the end, they'll wonder who could give them such a sunny do?
Celebs are always on the move, not much time to groove!

Natasha Nuttall (12)

Nature And Its Months

Nature, it's a wonderful thing
Like a gold or silver ring
Nature is a beautiful thing
Like bells going *ting, ting, ting*
Nature is a lovely thing
Like the bird, soft beat of its wing

January's for the birds that sing
February, is for everything
March, is the month for the kings
Then comes April when things start to grow
May, is when winter knows it's time to go
June, is not the time to sow
July, here comes the heat, oh no!
August, the heat is here when I stand along the pier
September is when summer knows the end is near
October, I saw it like a seer
November, it's the coldest month of the year
December, Christmas is here and so is the new year.

Clare Astle (12)

The Wind

The wind is powerful,
Flying, jumping, rising,
Rattling, battering,
Ploughing through the cities.

Destroying homes,
Crashing, banging,
The wind whacking through,
Whooshing, playing in the fields.

Bending trees, breaking bridges,
Twisting, turning, dipping,
Blowing twigs, whooshing past our ears,
The wind.

Nathan Goddard (13)

My Family

It's been four years since he has lived with me,
He has hurt my family including me,
Over the years he caused such pain,
Yet he has a certain touch,
A touch in my life so as I can't leave him,
He will always be in my heart,
This is my father.

She was there for me all the time,
She eased my fear, felt my pain,
She gave me hope in my life,
I never want to hurt her,
We love her and she loves us,
This is my mother.

When my mum wasn't there, she was
She held my hand when I was shaken,
We shared our thoughts and our dreams,
She was naughty, I was innocent,
I cried, she cried,
This is my sister.

In times of hassle and heartache,
I feel such strength surrounding me,
With all your love, I will accomplish all in life,
I love you all, my family.

Jennifer Kirkham (12)

My Fluffy Friend

Hop, skip, jump,
My fluffy little lump.

Snuggled up in the day,
Resting in its warm hay.

It has long ears which are nice and brown,
When it's sad they hang right down.

It spends all day chomping away,
Then goes to sleep in the hay
And sleeps till the next day.

Carrot is its favourite meal,
It hopes Safeway have a good deal.

My fluffy friend is the best,
It's better than all the rest.

Laura Arrowsmith (12)

My Stranger

There's someone sitting next to me,
He walks with me as well,
No matter where I go,
He's always near me.
I feel I know him in my heart,
But in my head I don't.
He might be related
Or he just might not,
But I wish I could find out,
Just who this person is.
But if I don't, what matters is,
I know he's in my heart,
He's with me forever and ever.

Shannon Barclay (12)

Puppy

Rich dark brown and soft as silk,
He sleeps upon the rug,
The brand new puppy is so cute,
Although he is a thug.

He fools you with his wagging tail
And gentle smiling face,
He shreds the paper, chews the shoes
And thinks he owns the place.

He digs down deep into the ground,
To find a tasty bone,
He has a massive appetite,
Weighs in at twenty stone!

He calls you with his yap, yap, yap
And drives you round the bend,
But all he ever really wants
Is just to be your friend.

Rachel Bennett (13)

The Moon

The moon is bright,
It watches over you at night.

When you're asleep in bed,
It watches over your head.

It's big and round,
It makes no sound.

It goes to sleep in the day,
It looks after you in every way.

When I'm asleep I never weep,
I know the moon's watching over me,
So I don't make a peep.

Hannah Oliver (13)

Extraterrestrial

They're coming, they're coming,
With green and flashing lights,
They're coming, they're coming,
You best keep out of sight.

They're coming, they're coming,
They're flying overhead,
They're coming, they're coming,
They'll get you in your bed.

They're coming, they're coming,
Your cows will disappear,
They're coming, they're coming,
They'll probe you in your ear.

They're coming, they're coming,
They want our planet now,
They're coming, they're coming,
Can we stop them? Yes, but how?

James Crossley (14)

What Are We? Just Guess!

We can fall to the ground
And twirl around,
We're as white as white can be
And the sky's as clear as the sea.
What are we? Just guess!

We can fall onto your face,
As your heart's at fast pace.
We're in different types of shapes,
We glisten with lots of shades,
What are we? Just guess!

Victoria Short-Sloman (13)

My Poem

You are
A shining star,
Nobody can hold you down,
You're the brightest
Star around.
Not one comment can
Get in your way
Because you're feeling
Good today,
So hold your head high
In the sky
And let the people shout
Hooray!

Natacha Bland (13)

Time

Turning and turning,
The wheels go round,
Backwards and forwards,
Round and round,
Synchronisation
Is the key,
Complete simplicity,
Always on time,
We never would be,
Without this accessory,
On my wrist I tell the time,
What would I be
Without my *father time*?

Ryan Gilfoyle (13)

Fear

Standing there on the stage,
In front of many people,
Staring as they gasp.

Standing there on the stage,
Her legs begin to shake
And she starts to sweat.

Standing there on the stage,
Looking for a signal,
Turning her head and searching.

Standing there on the stage,
Looking at everyone in the crowd,
As they turn their heads and whisper.

Standing there on the stage,
Someone shouted, 'Get on with it.'
She goes red and turns towards the door.

Standing there on the stage,
She begins to panic,
Wondering whether to run or not.

Standing there on the stage,
Having no choice but to run and cry,
Everyone stands up and begins to laugh.

Marianne Kenny (13)

Death By Part

I feel not living nor dead,
The hairs that stand up in cold air,
Pain like fire burning in the head,
The pain lies ahead is hard not fair.

The weight on my shoulders that weighs me down,
Heart dead as if split in two,
Thinking to myself all alone,
Brain mixed up like an untied shoe.

Place of cold shivers,
Your heart freezes like ice,
Trembling and sickness in your livers,
The floor is covered with tiny mice.

Each day seems to never end,
Pain I suffer from every fight,
A sword which I shall lend,
Blood is spilled every red clouded night.

Leigh Kinder (13)

No More Pain

The rain's coming down on me,
Washes my troubles away,
The rain's coming down on me,
No tears, no pain, no way.

When I check my answer phone,
No message to say that you're gone,
I miss you so much it's untrue,
But I'll get over you.

Why did our love just die?
Just answer me, tell me why,
I miss you so much it's untrue,
But I'll get over you.

Dannii Winstanley (13)

Storm

Leaves twirling way up high,
Umbrellas swirling in the sky,
Trees sway side to side,
Cats and dogs run away and hide.

Rain bouncing off the ground,
Cars turning round and round,
Trees falling on the floor,
Rain begins to pour and pour.

Little babies start to cry,
They don't know what's happening
And they don't know why.

The leaves fall with ease,
As they float in the gentle breeze,
Now the storm has ended,
Everything is mended.

Liz Winkley (13)

The Wind!

As I lay in bed at night,
I hear the wind blow,
Sometimes it scares me so.

As I walk to school,
I hear the wind blow,
Rustling all the leaves so I watch them go.

On the way home from school
I don't hear the wind blow
It must have gone to bed, I think to myself as I go.

Time to go to bed
And I hear the wind blow,
Now I know it scares me so.

Kathryn Mulligan (13)

Driving In The Car

We're driving in the car
And we're going really quick,
'Dad slow down,
I'm feeling really sick!'

I wind down the window,
To get a bit of air,
'Quick, do it back up!
Now look at my hair!'

'Are we nearly there yet?'
'Stop whinging in the back!'
Another half an hour, I bet,
I grabbed a book from the rack.

The road is very bumpy,
My stomach's feeling jumpy.
I hope we get there soon,
Before I start to swoon.

We're slowing down at last,
I can't believe we're here,
My sickness has passed,
Have I been a pain in the rear?

Amy Willis (13)

Rain

Rain, rain, the constant fall,
The patter of the windowpane,
Like an army, the drops invade,
The night as tiny soldiers.

The heavens open and drop to Earth,
The water beats the ground,
Soldiers calm and cease their fire,
Sun shines through like a torch.

Henry Graham (14)

Poem

Our lives aren't close to victory
We need to change the course of history
Everyone of us needs a miracle
Most of us need something biblical
The world's full of emergency
We've all got a sense of urgency

All of the motion left inside
And the memories all tied
Let hope grow in your eyes
Doesn't matter about your heart's size
You think you're good but a few years later
I'm pretty sure you'll end up as a waiter

I don't care what you've done
I don't like what you've become
And all of your lies
Could fill the shires
But is this how I'd want to be
Because freedom comes naturally?

Robert Pocock (13)

Water

It splashes; it crashes,
It spills; it pours,
It trickles; it sprinkles
And cascades past boat oars.

It flows as it travels,
Fast down the stream,
It twists and it turns,
Like storms in a dream.

It's life-giving yet deadly –
Too little, too much,
It's smooth, it's rapid,
Right down to the touch.

Hannah Eyres (14)

The Bus

As the bus pulls up, the engine rumbles,
Of the thought of going to school
My stomach tumbles

On we pile
The bus driver smiles
I hand him my fare
Then give him a stare
I stumble to my seat
'Cause I nearly fall over my feet

As we pull up at the next stop
I can see the corner shop
There's boys and girls about
'Come on, we'll be late,' we all shout

As we pull up at school
Some pupils start acting the fool
Then the bus driver shouts
'Come on, everyone out!'

Laura Whatmough (13)

My Winter's Walk

I walk along a grassy bank,
the wind is all around.
I hear the sound of crispy leaves,
falling to the ground.
As I look up at the sky,
I see snowflakes fall by.
They fall and fall to the ground,
if only I could hear the sound,
but instead I hear the sound of my feet scraping along the ground.
The air is cold, the wind is strong,
I keep on walking along and along.

Natalie Smith (14)

The Race

As I stand there my body shaking,
I went to bed last night,
With all the fears of me waking.
I stand at the start line
And wait for the sign.
I hear the bang of the gun,
My legs weigh a ton,
There is a roar of the crowd,
It is such a loud sound.
I pass the other people in the race,
As I steady my pace.
I see the tape getting closer,
My teacher asked me if I was going to win the race
And I said, 'No, Sir.'
I crossed the line and I came first,
My body nearly burst.

Laura Towers (13)

Winter's Movement

Winter's round the corner, it's my favourite time of year,
The trees start swaying in the wind, letting me know it's here,
The leaves drop off in a very strange way,
They flutter and swirl in the air, before racing down to the ground,.
Children are awaiting to toss them all around,
They cry with joy as they run about,
While waiting for the leaves to parachute down,
There is movement all around.
The children run and skip about to keep their bodies warm,
At night the ground starts moving the creatures come out to feed,
Another day is over, it's nearly time for sleep.
The children are all tucked up in bed,
As cosy as can be.
They dream of snowflakes falling and awaken with delight,
Winter is finally here.

John Fishwick (13)

Season Of Change

Winter has arrived
It comes once a year
It gets very cold
And white snow appears

It is the time of year when animals go and sleep
In the homes they have prepared
From the dead leaves
And sticks that they have gathered

Snowflakes scatter from the sky
Soaring down like beautiful doves
Children playing
Wearing hats and gloves

As the animals awake
And the children stop playing
The fun is over
And the snowflakes stop relaying

It is the end of winter
All the snow has gradually gone
The sun is shining down
And now summer is upon.

Richard Mitchell (13)

Christmas Time

On Christmas Eve, I am as happy as anyone can be,
Staring at the presents beneath the Christmas tree.

Wrapping paper, tinsel, Christmas card galore,
Comet, Dasher, Prancer, Rudolph and even more.

Rudolph and his shiny nose shining through the sky,
It's nearly midnight, Santa will very soon be flying by.

Christmas Day has come and gone and so have Santa's friends,
New Year's Day will soon be here, the excitement officially ends.

Gabrielle Barrow (13)

Rock 'N' Roller Coaster

Huge, vibrant lights flashing
Long carriages, colours dashing
Loud music from above

Quick rapid sudden move
Stretched rattling carriages groove
Terrified white knuckles

Flicking, twisting, turning
Plummeting down, stomach's churning
Up, down and round and round

Speeding round, rising fears
Deafening music, thumping ears
Screeching screams from behind

Near end, not too easy
Never again, feelin' queasy
Stand clear, *blaaah!*

Jennie Harrap (13)

Swim Race

Everyone was watching, or so it seemed,
My goal was to win, it's what I always dreamed.
Standing frozen at the edge of the pool,
I started to shiver, I felt like a fool.

I dived in the water and glided to the top,
My heart was pounding, I thought it might stop.
I pushed myself forward and gave it my all,
Just a few more strokes and I may reach the wall.

I couldn't believe it, I was finally there,
But was I the winner? It was too much to bear!
I'd trained for this moment for months on end,
Sacrificed so much, I almost went round the bend.
The judges were talking, they couldn't agree,
The suspense was amazing, then they all looked at me!

Amanda Smart (14)

Darkness

It fell, silently at first

The sun shyly hid her face
Behind the tallest of the trees
Her rays scattering like the branches
Sent dancing in the breeze
But soon the dappled patterns faded
And the shadows standing tall
Slowly faltered, slumped and shrank
Leaving only grey covering all
A black blanket drifted down
And the dark shadow that was cast
Smothered all the land
Night had arrived at last

And a girl danced, bathed in moonlight
On silver sands by a foaming sea
Her hair shimmering as she twirled
For in the darkness she is free.

Paula Mearns (14)

The Wind

The wind is a wild untamed beast,
Rapidly moving from west to east.
Surging and roaring ready to rage,
Fierce like a lion locked up in a cage.

In violent and anger, rocking the trees,
Scaring young children, would it stop, please.
Paper and litter flying around,
It almost lifts people from the ground.

After the wind has let off its steam,
Calmer and quieter, or so it seems.
We now only feel a light gentle breeze,
Because the wind now feels at ease.

Sophie Bradley (14)

The Flight

Ready for take-off; shot up from the ground,
Faster than the speed of light,
Ears making quite a sound,
Families all around me,
Having so much fun,
We're going on our holidays,
Towards the winter sun.

As my eyes took to the window
And many clouds passed by,
I saw a great big dolphin,
Waving from the sky.
To my left beams of light
Shot up from through the clouds,
Shining directly in my eyes,
I pulled the shutter down.

And then to my surprise,
Over the tannoy a booming voice arose,
Making me jump out of my skin,
'Could all the crew please take their seats'
And I quickly jumped back in.

Time to put my belt back on,
As the nose began to slope,
Joyful faces all around,
Excitement, joy and hope,
Before I knew it we hit the ground,
My stomach in my mouth.
We'd reached our destination
And my heart began to pound.

Aimee Callaghan (14)

An Autumn Breeze

Over and under,
Through and about,
She floats on a cloud,
Magnificent throughout.

A breeze of autumn,
Like a shower of spring,
Leaves by the thousand,
Does the autumn wind bring.

A chariot riding,
On high in the air,
Scattered all over,
As the ground's golden hair.

Broken underfoot,
With a sharp crisp crunch,
A horse on the gallop,
Blown by the bunch.

For months on end
The soldiers fall,
But the generals stand,
Still proud and tall.

The battlefields lie,
Scattered with dead,
The grass interrupted,
By gold, brown and red,

Soon the war will be over,
When winter arrives
And a blanket of snow
Hides leaves that have died.

Grant Gallacher (14)

The Daily Train

The awaited train pulls in at the station,
Out spew the mums, dads and that distant relation,
Fanning out like a peacock's feather,
In compass directions and not together,
The clip of high heels, the clatter of feet,
As some leave the station onto the street.

The anticipated passengers eagerly get on,
Shoppers, people with suitcase, one by one,
The businessmen, smart, neat-suited in black,
Read their newspapers at the back.

Speeding along past handkerchief fields,
As fast as advancing armies with swords and shields.
Houses whizz past with all kinds of colours,
Different sizes and shapes with windows and shutters,
There is a mill and there a river,
Each a glimpse and gone forever.

Elliot Lavin (14)

Your Choice

I am the daughter you willingly chose not to know,
No older than one was I, and away you stole.
14 years today and still no word from you, Dad,
Did you ever miss me? Are you ever secretly sad?
Do you ever miss me and want to ask, 'How was school, Love?'
Want to dry my tears when I cry and give a warm comforting hug?
Have you ever questioned yourself for what you did that day?
Birthdays and Christmas, no card off Daddy, another year in dismay.
So I go on wondering who you were and what's become of you now?
I dwell upon wanting to know, did you ever dare to doubt?
I look deep into the only picture, I possess of you,
But this my only knowledge of you, so what am I supposed to do?
I cannot find the courage to meet you, send you a letter or
talk on the phone,
So forever I'm the daughter you choose willingly not to have known.

Amy O'Farrell (14)

Nothing More To Say

As the night grew dim we clasped our hands
And looked into each other's eyes,
Taking one step left, then another to the right,
As we glided to either side.

The train on my dress flowed across the floor,
So delicate and so smooth,
We drew ourselves closer
And gracefully began to move.

Such a beautiful dance it was,
It spoke a thousand words,
For any couple seen to be doing this dance,
Were to be seen as committed lovebirds.

Trying hard not to tread on one another's toes,
We smiled and increased our pace,
The limelight was dimming, the moonlight peeking in,
This place was filled with so much grace.

The music was imaginary,
But we could hear it in our heads,
Nobody was around,
But the birds in the trees overhead.

We gradually slowed down as we lightly pushed ourselves away,
The dance had said it all,
There was nothing more to say.

Caroline Hill (14)

Emotional Movement

Messed up in the heart
Messed up in the head
Don't want to be apart
Just wish I was dead

Things that always happen
Seem to mean not much
When I lay here craving
Every single touch

Dreading every morning
Dreading what they'll say
Scared to get out of bed
Scared to start the day

Worried about the room they have
Worried about going home
Frightened to leave the classroom
Frightened of where they roam

Ready to leave this world
Ready to wish it all away
For me yet more torture
For them just another day.

Michael Knight (14)

Lonely Tree

As it rustles like a hedge in winter,
Its brown, crinkly leaves shake,
As it almost stares at your for days,
As if it's going to awake,
The lonely tree.

It's a lonely tree, all cold and damp,
As it looks so soft and still,
It's so quiet with little sound,
Still standing,
The lonely tree.

The tree is faded, like it's art,
As it rains, it looks like tears,
It's a lonely tree with no fears,
It changes colours with different seasons,
Why the tree is there, it has no reasons.

The tree is so harmless
And so heart touching too,
It's so calm to the people around,
To the tree; *everything makes a loud sound*,
The lonely tree.

Jackson Hall (14)

The Quiet Child

Her soul is tired
Her faith is weak
Her heart is on fire
But still she's trying to seek
The quiet child is helpless

Her body's full of bruises
Her heart is full of pain
Will this torture ever ease
Guess not, there's that fist again
The quiet child has not a friend

She's always helping others
Always there for them
No one seems to care, not even her mother
Everyone ignores her being nasty like them
The quiet child's pain is excruciating

She is always hanging on to tomorrow
Wondering what will happen next
Living with hurt and sorrow
Her heart like an airtight sack
The quiet child wants to die

She can't take another thump
Another word from their lips
Another bone on the floor, bump!
She's crying as her clothes rip
The quiet child has taken enough.

She decides to end it all,
To be happy and free,
Oh no there she falls,
Like the Titanic in the sea,
The quiet child suffers no more.

Anne-Marie Sane (16)

Vehicles

Speed of fire,
Enormous tyre,
Posh a Bentley,
Use it gently,
As common as Rover,
Which gets you to Dover,
Fast as a rocket car,
It gets you far,
Alfa Romeo,
Has a stereo,
As good as Zonda,
Same as Honda,
Just like Nissan,
It doesn't have a fan,
Mitsubishi's nice,
It drives more than twice,
Ferrari spider,
Is a good rider,
Just like a BM,
It is worth more than a gem,
Audi TT's small,
But it can destroy a brick wall,
Lamborghini's fast,
It won't let anything get past,
Tank is strong,
There is nothing wrong,
The fastest motorbike is Suzuki,
If you have it, don't get too keen,
Doors of steel,
Suits the wheel.

Zeeshan Akhtar (12)

Christmas

Christmas tree in the room, lights all around
Presents under the tree
The lovely smell of turkey
The white blanket of snow outside
People laughing all around
People playing outside
Bang!
Snowball hits the window
The next day comes
Where the presents are open
Paper all around
Children run off to ring their friends
The games are played
The food is eaten
Father Christmas has gone for another year.

Nathan Shackell (13)

Animals

What I love about animals is the way they differ from each other,
What I hate about animals is when they die.

What I love about lions is their roar,
What I hate about lions is their fearlessness.

What I love about cats is their playfulness,
What I hate about cats is their claws.

What I love about tigers is their stripes,
What I hate about tigers is their growl.

What I love about owls is their great wiseness,
What I hate about owls is their hoot.

What I love about animals is the way they differ from each other,
What I hate about animals is when they die.

Rebecca Lenton (12)

Mixed Feelings

People are stuck with it
They learn to live with it
Disease
I hate that stuff

Some people are addicted to it
Doctors predicted they will die from it
Drugs
I hate that stuff

Some people are scared of it
They learn to live with it
Spiders
I hate that stuff

Every religion has it
People celebrate it
Festivals
I like that stuff

Everyone has it
You can't get enough of it
Happiness
I like that stuff

Everyone watches it
You can't miss it
EastEnders
I like that stuff

Everyone has to eat it
You can't live without it
Chocolate
I like that stuff

Everyone likes and dislikes stuff
They have to live with it,
Whether you like it or not.

Jinal Patel (13)

Make-Up

Oh no, no make-up left
What's the time?
Just enough time
Grab my bag
Grab my purse
Rush to the shops
The shop doors open
We rush in
Going straight down the isle
There we see
All the cosmetics
Shimmering pinks, gold and silver
Eyeshadows of every colour
Pitch-black, light brown and clear
Mascaras in every size
Slashes of lilac, blue and silver
Bottled in every size
We rush to the till
Before it closes
Oh no
Checkout closes
Too late
Oh well
Maybe we'll come back next time!

Meera Samani (14)

Stuff

The Earth is covered with it,
Gardens are smothered with it,
Grass,
I like that stuff.

Everyone gets bored by it,
Everyone has to put up with it,
School,
I hate that stuff.

People like playing it,
People break their ankles by it,
Hockey,
I like that stuff.

People take drugs with it,
Sometimes you need it,
Injections,
I hate that stuff.

You can spend ages on it,
It's annoying when you can't do it,
PS2 games,
I like that stuff.

Girls always do it,
Boys can never put up with it,
Giggling,
I hate that stuff.

Joshua Partridge (13)

Stuff!

Most people unwrap presents at it
Some of us eat pheasants at it
Christmas
I like that stuff

Too many people die from it
Pain is always there with it
Disease
I hate that stuff

People fall in it
They don't want to fall out of it
Love
I like that stuff

People squirm at them
You would get lots of germs without them
Injections
I hate that stuff.

Christina Whittam (13)

Birthdays

I like birthdays,
Now I'm one year older,
Now I've got one year less,
I've got lots of presents,
I've had lots of fun,
I've got lots of clothes,
I've got lots of money,
All my family come round,
But now that I'm older
I get less and less,
But it happens to everyone,
But I'm not bothered,
I still love birthdays.

Michael Reynolds (14)

I Hate That Stuff

People die of it,
Lots of people have it,
Cancer,
I hate that stuff.

Addicts live for it,
People die from it,
Drugs,
I hate that stuff.

Close ones cry at it,
People live in it,
Graveyards,
I hate that place.

Kids are terrified of it,
Often men go to jail for it,
Paedophilia,
I hate that stuff.

People are scarred by it,
Living things die of it,
Fire,
I hate that stuff.

Leanne Reed & Craig Mitchell (13)

Music

Elvis, Korn, Slipknot, rock
Kylie, SClub, Busted, pop
Jay-z, Nas, D-12, hip-hop
Old, classic, opera, country
Rhymes, beats, songs, poetry
Accapella, instrumental, you choose it
It's all one thing, we call it music.

Louis Carnegie (13)

War

Gun goes bang
Bang goes boom
Boom makes war
What is this for?

The meaning of war
Bring destruction and more
Crying and dying
What is this for?

Land power
Selfish, greed
The option of war
Thunders down, more and more

Bombs, guns, slaughtering more
Allies, enemies, bringers of war
Death and destruction
Developing more and more.

Lewis Hunt (12)

Shopping

'See you later,'
Slamming the door,
Shopping, shopping, never a bore.
New Look, Select, HMV,
Searching, searching, what will I see?
Shops, shops with bargains galore,
All I can think about is shopping some more,
With my friends we walk around,
Hunting for bargains waiting to be found,
Claire's Internaçional and Mark 1,
Shopping with mates is loads of fun,
When we have no more money to spend
The shopping day comes to an end.

Perri Ross (12)

Love Is . . .

Love is an emotion
The strongest around

Love is patient
Blind and true

Love is kisses
Me and you

Love is red roses
Strawberries and cream

Love is hurtful
Hatred and cheats

Love is not boastful
Rude or selfish

Love is family
Marriage and kids

Love is us
Together, forever.

Sara Humphries (12)

War

War . . . war
Is peace going
To have its turn
Everybody will learn
That war will burn

War is everywhere
Conjuring up deaths
In its lair

If only war ended
And peace began
Then everybody will
Give war a ban.

Gary Clelland (13)

I Love . . .

I love . . .
Rainy days
Sunshine rays
Making snowmen
School holidays

I love . . .
Christmas mornings
Just waking up
Birthday presents
Mini Easter eggs in a cup

I love . . .
To shop until I drop
I'm always down town
Where balloons go pop
Always wipes away my frown

I love . . .
Strawberry laces
Sugar mice
Fudge in cases
They all taste so nice.

Sarah Frith (12)

BMXing

High jumping
Fast pumping
Big air
Windy hair
Big bumps
Heavy jumps
Bar spinning
Twinned-wheels spinning
Fast flips
High tricks.

Tom Brady (13)

Entertainment

Bowl the ball
Hit the wickets
This boring game
It's cricket

Hit the ball
Over the net
Tennis is fun
I'll beat him yet

Tim Henman
Is the headman
Tiger Woods
Is the hit man

David Beckham
England squad
Man United's
Mini god.

Joe Nield (12)

Christmas Eve

The day before our big day, that's Christmas Eve,
The Christmas tree lights are bright, filling the whole room,
My mum is busy thinking and planning ahead
For the forthcoming day,
Dad stocking presents under the tree
And getting ready for any guests,
We are sent to bed but too excited to sleep,
We lay there thinking of what we will receive on Christmas Day,
We hear guests coming and are not sure
What presents they have bought,
But slowly, slowly, slowly we drift off to sleep
And wait to see what happens.

Emma Sayles (13)

Love Is . . .

Your smile so sweet,
I forget what I'm doing,
Trip over my feet.

I get a feeling inside,
My heart pounds so much,
My sadness turns to pride.

He is good looking and fine,
I have one wish,
'I hope he'll be mine.'

I don't know what to say,
Every time I'm near you,
The words just drift away.

When you're cuddling all day long,
Love is true
And never wrong.

I love you with my heart,
I love you with my soul,
All with a love I can't control.

I will never forget you, even when I die,
You have also hurt my feelings
And you made me cry.

What does this all mean?
Am I in love?
Or is this just a dream?

Chelsey Wager (13)

Friday Nights, Saturday Mornings

It's that funny feeling you get,
The relief of knowing it's Saturday,
Waking up in the morning,
To the bright sunshine in May.

You fall back to sleep,
Underneath your covers,
You won't be waking up
For a few more hours.

You're tired from last night,
You went to your best mate's house,
When you get back home,
You curl up like a mouse.

It gets to 11 o'clock,
The morning air smells sweet,
You decide to get up,
Back up on your feet.

It gets to Monday morning,
The air is dark and cold,
The alarm clock blares away,
'Get up,' I am told.

Going to bed on a Friday night,
Is something I love to do,
When you wake in the morning,
You feel so brand new.

Lauren Perkins (13)

Love Is . . .

Love is you
Love is me
Love is happy as can be

Love is beautiful
Love is alive
Send me Cupid for £5.95

Love is patient
Love is kind
Love is stuck at the back of my mind

Love is a fantasy
Love is a desire
When I'm with you my heart's on fire

Love is passionate
Love is potions
Love is having happy emotions

Love is romance
Love is together
Love will always be forever.

Hollie Rossiter (12)

Presents

Sparkling paper, many bows,
One by one, stacked in colourful rows,
People coming, handing out pressies,
This year from Nan, another pair of wellies.

Big ones, small ones,
Waiting to be opened,
As well as people coming and giving and giving,
Making sure they're not living.

Spending Christmas money in town,
Christmas pudding, third around.

Natasha Hamirani (13)

Teenagers

Painful puberty
All day through
Loving food
And fizzy drinks too
Hating school
And being rude
Doing what's cool
But always in a mood
Always growing
Talking on the phone
Spells of arguing
Having a moan
Alcohol and drugs
Smoking too
Turning into thugs
Getting what's new
Choosing what to wear
Dreaming about actors
Greasy hair
That's most teenagers!

Bina Patel (12)

The Thoughts Of A Toy

Once I was the treasure of treasures,
King of the toys,
Ruler,
I was the warrior of warriors,
But then . . .
My leg broke,
It wouldn't fix,
Now I'm in the broken bag,
Locked away,
I must escape,
I must escape.

Ali Sayed (14)

Love Is . . .

Love is happiness
Love is kind
It's really very hard to find

Love is passion
Love is kissing
It's something everyone is missing

Love is romance
Love is forever
It's you and me always together

Love is alive
Love is families
It's all the happy memories

Love is treasured
Love is a fire
It fills your heart with desire

Love is beautiful
Love is blind
It hurts you so many times.

Lorren Lawton (13)

Bullies

They punch and they kick,
They call you names like thick,
They swear and act hard,
Then they go home in a sports car.

The next day they come back,
Then they chuck you in a sack,
Then they make you feel like poo,
Then they scare by shouting *boo*.

But in the end they go away,
But the bully says, 'See you in May.'

Matthew Merison (12)

I Love . . .

Walking through the rain,
Getting soaked and feeling no pain,
Soaking up the sunshine's rays,
How I love the summer days.
Making snowmen is such fun,
Snow looking like icing on an iced bun.

I love . . .
Going shopping to the town,
My friends and me always go down.
I really can't stop until I drop.
Soon about to run out of money,
Got to go home in a hurry.

I love . . .
Waking up and getting the holiday feeling,
Jumping up nearly touching the ceiling.
Can't wait to get into the car
And at night watching the twinkling stars,
To a hotel, where we will stay,
Finally somewhere to lay.

I love . . .
Christmas trees,
Mistletoe please,
Crackers galore,
Presents, more,
Santa hats
And fluffy cats!

Charlotte Parry (12)

The Race

Starting gun,
People run.

People passing,
Colours rushing.

Runners panting,
Hearts thumping.

People falling,
Knees are grazing.

People screaming,
Runners rising.

The thunder of feet,
As people sit in their seat.

People staring,
As they're cheering.

Finishing line,
Stop the time.

Team won,
No more run.

Peter Reynolds (12)

When It Snows

When it snows, it snows for me,
Jumping and running,
I'm crazy as can be.

When all my friends bring a surprise,
Really it's just a pile of snow
Going into my eyes.

As evening comes,
We all get chilly, cold bums,
Wearing our favourite pink fluffy thongs.

Drinking warm cocoa,
Snow has come and gone
And left to see it none.

When it snows, it snows for me,
This is the best day that can be.

Rebecca Arksey (12)

Pollution

Pollution here we go
You can see it flow
Thrown through the street
Binmen picking up the cans
Pollution from the vans
Looking at our local stream
Trolleys, bins, baker's cakes
Flowing with the decayed cream
Pollution did this to our old beautiful stream
But you can help it go
All you have to do is say no
When you're about to drop something
On the street floor
Just help a little more.

Jason Stephens (12)

Truth

People volunteer for it,
Others shed a tear for it,
War,
I hate that stuff.

Children have nightmares about it,
Others don't seem to care about it,
School,
I hate that stuff.

Half the world does wrong for it,
The other half longs for it,
Money,
I hate that stuff.

They're gonna get relegated,
Alan Smith is overrated,
Leeds,
I hate that stuff.

America is unaware of it,
The rest of the world is scared of it,
Pollution,
I really hate that stuff.

Asa Masters (13)

I Love . . .

Walking through the rain,
Getting soaked and feeling no pain,
Soaking up the sunshine's rays,
How I love the summer days.
Making snowmen is such fun,
Snow looking like icing on an iced bun.

I love . . .
Going shopping to the town,
My friends and me always go down.
I really can't stop until I drop.
Soon about to run out of money,
Got to go home in a hurry.

I love . . .
Waking up and getting the holiday feeling,
Jumping up nearly touching the ceiling.
Can't wait to get into the car
And at night watching the twinkling stars,
To a hotel, where we will stay,
Finally somewhere to lay.

I love . . .
Christmas trees,
Mistletoe please,
Crackers galore,
Presents, more,
Santa hats
And fluffy cats!

Charlotte Parry (12)

The Race

Starting gun,
People run.

People passing,
Colours rushing.

Runners panting,
Hearts thumping.

People falling,
Knees are grazing.

People screaming,
Runners rising.

The thunder of feet,
As people sit in their seat.

People staring,
As they're cheering.

Finishing line,
Stop the time.

Team won,
No more run.

Peter Reynolds (12)

Love And Hate

I hate it when we argue
I love it when we make up
I hate it when you tell me I'm wrong
I love it when I'm right
I hate it when you tease me
I love it when you hug me
I hate it when you're not there
I love it when I get time alone
I hate it when you blame me
I love it when you say sorry
I hate it when I'm lonely
I love it when you come back
I hate it when you laugh at me
I love it when you smile
I hate it when you ignore me
I love it when you tell me things
I hate it when I cannot sleep
I love it when you haunt my dreams
I hate you
I love you.

Eloise Bullen (13)

Red

Red,
The colour of anger,
Lights on the Christmas tree.
Red,
The colour of language books,
Not the lessons for me.
Red,
The colour of danger,
A loved one's gift of a rose.
Red,
The colour of love,
Nail varnish on my toes.
Red,
The colour of cherries,
Rosy apples too.
Red,
The colour of berries,
Is this the colour for you?

Danielle Beetson (13)

I Love You!

Roses are red,
Violets are blue,
Love is me lovin' you.

Violets are purple,
Roses are pink,
When I'm without you, I just can't think.

Love is you,
Love is me,
Love is crazy as can be.

But all
I can say is
I love you . . .

Lencia Ryan (12)

Pressies

As the sun rises
Surprises, surprises

It's my birthday

Birthday cake
That I like to make

So much food
It puts me in a groovy mood

When pressies come
I can't wait any longer
Especially the one from my mum

As friends knock on the door
Lots and lots more

The day is over and it won't
Be my birthday anymore

Birthday cake is all gone
I love my new pink thong

I wish it was my birthday again
I think I will go out and play with Ben.

Kirsty Adams (12)

Why Sadness . . .

Tears twisting,
Listening,
Blotchy eyes,
As they die,
The soft moaning, like a haunting ghost,
A sad letter through the post,
Tears running,
Shotguns gunning,
The wondering they ask:
'Is she laughing or crying?'
People lying
In all the foreign parts,
Suffering and dying and living in carts,
Dying with hunger and thirst,
People thinking they can go first,
Newborn babies crying,
Rich people lying.

Why sadness . . .

Jemma Waite (13)

Christmas Poem

I can't get to sleep,
Waiting for the day to come,
What will my presents be?
Will they be nice?
The noises downstairs,
I was hoping for a computer,
New roller skates
And a knew bike,
Like prisoners locked up,
I am so excited about Christmas,
Now that Christmas is over,
I feel sad and extremely fat,
After eating all of that food.

Alysha Vaghela (13)

Firework Display

F laming rockets
I n fireworks is gunpowder
R eally big bangs and sparks
E veryone is happy
W onderful colours
O range, yellow and red
R eady for the grand finale
K ebab and burger for sale

D ark night
I ndigo and violet shine in the sky
S ilver and gold
P urple and blue
L ong whistle before a wonderful display
A re you ready?
Y ou are so happy, you dance all night long.

Alexander Brown (12)

Sport

Round and smooth
Fancy patterns and designs
Easy to kick, soft and bouncy
Curls through the air
Shines like a star
That's a football

Red and rock hard
Easy to hit 4s and 6s
Fast and easy to get people out
That's a cricket ball

Shaped just like an egg
Spins over the bar and gets 3 points
Easy to kick and always scores
That's a rugby ball.

Ashley Roberts (12)

I Love . . . I Hate . . .

I love it when the sky turns blue,
I hate it when it starts to rain,
I love it when I lay in the sun,
I hate it when I'm in pain,
I hate it when my skin goes red,
I love it if it goes brown,
I hate it when I start to peel,
I love it when the sun don't frown,
I love it when I get to swim,
I hate it when I float,
I love it when I'm underwater,
I hate it when on a boat,
I hate it when I go home,
I love it when I sleep,
I hate it when I fall out of bed,
I love it on the beach,
I love it when the sun is setting,
I hate it when it's gloomy,
I love it when there's sand on my shoes,
I hate it when it's *stormy!*

Genna Bradbury (13)